MONEY OUT LOUD

MONEY OUT LOUD

ALL THE FINANCIAL STUFF NO ONE TAUGHT US

BERNA ANAT

Quill Tree Books
An Imprint of HarperCollinsPublishers

Quill Tree Books is an imprint of HarperCollins Publishers.

Money Out Loud
Text copyright © 2023 by Berna Anat
Illustrations by Monique Sterling

Library of Congress Cataloging-in-Publication Data

Names: Anat, Berna, author.
Title: Money out loud : all the financial stuff no one taught us / by Berna Anat.
Description: First editon. | New York, NY : Quill Tree Books, [2023] |
Audience: Ages 13 up | Audience: Grades 10–12 | Summary: "In this nonfiction
    teen book, 'financial hype woman' Berna Anat explains all the stuff young
    adults need to know about personal finance, covering everything from how
    and why to make a budget, to understanding the inequalities of our economy
    and how to work to change them"— Provided by publisher.
Identifiers: LCCN 2022020978 | ISBN 9780063067370 (hbk.)
    | ISBN 9780063067363 (pbk.)
Subjects: LCSH: Money—Juvenile literature. | Finance, Personal—Juvenile
    literature. | Budgets, Personal—Juvenile literature.
Classification: LCC HG221.5 .A52 2023 | DDC 332.4—dc23/eng/20220923
LC record available at https://lccn.loc.gov/2022020978

Typography by Monique Sterling
23 24 25 26 27 LBC 5 4 3 2 1

First Edition

*To the Mangubat Matriarchy and all who carry the machete—I mean,
the torch—especially Magdalena, Bema, Robie, Jasmine, Jordan,
Jada, Isla, and everyone who pops out after this.
Everything I do is for us.*

*Also, Mom?
This might be as close as you'll get re: a grandchild from me.
Pls gigil it accordingly.*

TABLE OF
CONTENTS

MIC CHECK

Ahem. Is this thing on?

So, question: Have you ever heard of a Financial Hype Woman? Probably not, because I friggin' made it up.

I'm Berna—I'm a financial educator, but more than that, I am a Financial Hype Woman. The whole point of a Hype Woman is to scream encouragement while you, the star, are doing your thing onstage.

So that's what I do, but money. You follow?

A Financial Hype Woman's job—which, again, I totally made up—is to remind you of your financial power. To keep your energy up so that you can stay center stage in your money life. To turn up the volume when you feel a little voiceless. A Hype Woman is also part of your support team—like, metaphorically, I'd help clean up when fans throw their bra at you, y'know? I got you.

But please believe: I wasn't always this loud about money.

A few years ago, I was just like the majority of Americans: drowning in my $38,000 of student debt and $12,000 of credit card debt. And as a Filipina American first-gen child of immigrants from a lower-income family with zero financial background, I was confused, embarrassed, and dehydrated. (From the crying.)

But when I finally hit the University of Googles and started teaching myself about money, I realized a bunch of stuff:

$ That too many "experts" gatekeep the information with super-confusing language

$ That our learned silence about money is keeping us in the dark (and keeping the gatekeepers rich)

$ And that finance in the US has the same freakin' problem as nearly every other industry: our money world is hella male, hella pale, and hella stale; BIPOC folks (Black, Indigenous & People of Color) have very few money experts to relate to.

There were basically no financial educators, authors, or creators who looked like me, who sounded like me—no one who even spoke Finance-ese in a way I could understand. It was all so dude-bro. So melanin-deficient. So SNORE.

Plus, financial education is barely taught in our school system, right? Sure, no one's necessarily keeping us off the internet for free, Google-able information. But I still needed to teach myself from scratch, on my own time—a massive privilege that not everyone has access to.

So, despite my own shame and complete lack of formal financial brainsmarts, I took the privilege I had and did my best to figure this $h*t out for myself. I used social media to document the money stuff I learned. I taught myself enough to pay off all my debt, build a savings, quit my job, travel the world for a year, and start a business. *financial hairflip*

Eventually, cool people took notice and asked me if I wanted to write about it. I promised myself I'd write the book I wish someone gave me when I was starting out. And that's what you're holding right now. Wild, right?!

In these pages, I get to yell out all my best Financial Hype Woman bangers based on everything I've learned, like:

- 🎤 You gotta unpack your financial trauma and rewrite your Money Story!
- 🎤 You can bust through financial anxiety by making these banks werk for you!
- 🎤 You can hack debt in a healthy way to live your actual best life!
- 🎤 You can help change the whole frickin' world with the dollars in your pocket!!

(Deep inhale) . . . but enough about me. We're here to take all these lessons and put *you* in the spotlight.

Maybe you picked up this book because your money sweats keep you from thriving. (I feel that.) Maybe you're pissed that no one taught you how to budget and instead filled your brain with all that whitewashed stuff they called "history." (Mmm.) Maybe you're not used to talking about money, because the whole world told you to keep money stuff on mute. (I MEAN.)

We're about to remix all that. There are things you can't control about money, and we'll talk all about it, but we'll mostly focus on the things you *can* control. We'll learn how to morph money from This Thing That Makes Your Pits Sweat to one of your most powerful life tools. And we'll learn the one truth missing from nearly every other piece of male/pale/stale financial education out there:

Learning about money can be hella fun.[1]

You don't need to have any type of financial background. All you gotta do is bring your whole self to the stage.

Let's get on with this show already, huh?

WHO IS THIS BOOK FOR?

Now, is this book for the Youths or the Olds? The answer, my boo, is Yes.

If you feel young, you belong here. You are CURRENTLY being failed by our financial education system. This book is everything they should have taught you when we were spending hours in the Mitochondria-Is-the-Powerhouse Education Era. This book is for you.

If you feel old, you belong here. You WERE failed by the financial education system, and then you were thrown into the world and expected to afford life anyway. Many of us "adults" are still young in our financial brains, except we've got that cute layer of money mistakes and trauma that we've already lived through. This book is for you.

This book is for the young and young-at-heart (like me) who are figuring it out; for those of us who don't have the privilege of simply forwarding confusing money stuff to our parents or asking the family's financial advisor for help. You're not alone anymore. You got me. You got us.

---

1 Fair warning: I use hella *hella* in this book. It's a slang term originating from BIPOC in the California Bay Area that basically means "very" or "a lot." You literally can't take the girl outta the Bay.

And this book is for every dark-skinned, big-haired, Othered kid out there in South City and Houston and Newark and Everywhere Else, wondering if they belong in this world—the finance one, or the bigger one.

Is there some way to avoid all the financial sad-a$$-ness that the Olds keep complaining about? Is money just all bad, forever? Or is there literally any other way to figure all this out?

Lemme rephrase my answer from up top: that's a hard yes.

HOW TO READ THIS BOOK

leans dramatically into mic, practically eats it ALL RIGHT, LISTEN. THIS IS NOT AN ALL-IN-ONE-SITTING TYPE OF BOOK. 'KAY?

You're holding, like, a decade's worth of basic financial education, plus the money brains of our incredible experts and community. You gotta take your time. If you don't, you'll get overwhelmed, maybe softly black out, and suddenly you're standing over a trash fire like a rabid raccoon and this book is evaporating in the flames. (I may or may not have had this fantasy after reading too many money books too quickly.)

That's why I included a **Wait, What?!** section at the end of each chapter, so you can always take a breath, and see what your next steps are. And that's why we included **Open Mic** sections to hear directly from folks like us in each chapter, so you know you're not alone in this thang.

Trust your brain when it says, "Dis tew much. We need

Netflix." Know that there's no "normal" timeline to learn this stuff—everyone's money journey is different, and lifelong. I'm not going anywhere, neither is this book, and for now, neither is capitalism (hayo!).

And, teeny reminder: I'm just your money-obsessed auntie/ cousin/bestie/weirdo who wants everyone to get financially free. For the serious, personal-to-you questions, you should always seek professional financial advice from someone like a Certified Financial Planner.

One last rule: You gotta have fun. I demand it. I require it. The whole point of this book is for you to enjoy your money and the things it unlocks for you. So if you aren't using the prompts and weird surprises and unnecessary footnotes in this book to have fun, then I will shut this show DOWN.

Okay. Can I get you some water? Did you eat?

Sweet. It's showtime. Let's go.

1

HELLA FEELINGS
(AKA YOUR MONEY STORY)

Mmm! First chapter. It always feels very first-day-of-school, right? If you're feeling ready as hell to learn the best quick tips of Good Money Management . . . pack it up. Cause we're not doing that yet. (And ew, I'd never call it ~money management~.)

Right now, what you're gonna need is something to write with, probably some Kleenex, and potentially a therapist on deck, because we're about to go deep.

Before we learn anything new, we gotta dig into what I call your Money Story. Your Money Story has very little to do with financial brainsmarts—it's all about your childhood, your history, and your personal feels. You, obviously, are the Main Character of your Money Story, and your backstory goes waaaay back.

According to a study by the University of Cambridge, we learn the majority of our basic money habits by age seven (!!). And by age nine, our understanding of money is more or less set in stone (!!!).

BRING IN THE SCIENCE!

Like, what?! I don't know about y'all, but no one was drilling me on Best Budgeting Practices at that age (or any age). Since hardly any of us are getting a formal financial education during those years (or any years), most of us actually form our earliest money habits through emotional context—through our everyday experiences in our childhood lives, with all of their joys and traumas.

Want some proof? Get cozy: my Money Story starts way before I was even born. (We see you, generational trauma!)

My (Mom's) Money Story

My mother, Bema—who has always known she's the Main Character, can I just say—was born in 1954 on Mindanao, a southern island in the Philippines. Raised by a single mother, she's the only daughter in a family of seven kids. Her province, Davao, barely had working electricity. So it was a big deal when one of the neighbors got a brand-new TV when my mom was around seven years old.

"We all watched him when he brought it from the street into his house," my mom said. "He made sure everyone could see."

Mom and her brothers were super jealous, of course; my lola (grandma in Tagalog) couldn't afford a TV. But the neighborhood kids quickly learned that Fancy TV Neighbor often watched TV with his window wide open. So they would all sneak up to his window and silently watch anything homeboy had on.

They did this every single afternoon—that is, until the neighbor caught them one day, screamed at them to go away, and slammed his windows shut.

Every time my mom tells this part of the story, her jaw clenches.

"I promised myself right then and there, standing at that window," she says, raising her finger. "I said to myself: One day, I'm going to grow up and go to America. I'm going to buy my own house. And I'm going to put a TV in every. Single. Room."

Like a bad bi$h, my mom eventually fulfilled her own promise: she did immigrate to America. She met my dad, a fellow immigrant, had us kids—and they did buy a house. And even though we were a lower-income household, we *did* grow up with a TV in nearly every room. (Most of those TVs were semi-crusty, second-hand joints that only got Channel 3, but she still *did that*.)

Now, my mom had told me this story countless times before. When I was growing up, it always sounded like your average "wHeN i wAs yOuR aGe" parental guilt trip. But after I started digging into my own financial feelings and history, my mom's story clicked for me in a totally different way.

It explained so much about why my mom sometimes bought expensive things on credit, even if we couldn't afford to pay it back.

It explained so much about why so many other Filipino immigrant families I knew put such an emphasis on showing off their new American wealth, no matter the cost.

And if I really thought about it, it explained so much about my own financial habits, the things I picked up from my parents—like the way I sometimes spent on things just to get that "I deserve this" feeling. Or how I often used to unload a whole paycheck on a few purchases, riding the adrenaline and fear that I'd never have that type of money again. I realized part of my mom's Money Story eventually became part of mine. It was like uncovering the origin story of a DC superhero.

Learning that my mom's TV revenge story aligns with the stuff she (accidentally) taught me about money blew my mind. But I also thought, is this just me, or is this a real thing? For everyone? Can science confirm?!

It's time to introduce you to my Textperts: my smart friends who are down to answer all the questions we've been too ashamed or confused to ask. And on the topic of money and feelings, there's no one better than Shani Tran: therapist, financial trauma warrior, and actual #TherapistTok hero (@theshaniproject).

holds up finger, grabs phone One sec.

SHANi TRAN

- SHE/HER
- LiCENSED PROFESSiONAL CLiNiCAL COUNSELOR
- HiLARiOUSLy iNFORMATiVE CONTENT CREATOR

TEXTSPERT

My beauty. I'm telling my readers that our earliest money memories really do affect us, but, uh... I'm obviously not a professional.

Could you please confirm??

Girl, don't get me on a rant 😁. Our earliest money memories really DO affect us, both mentally and physically.

Slap some facts on 'em so they know foreal!!

YUP. There's a science-based therapy practice called cognitive behavioral therapy (CBT) 🧠

Which explores the ways our thoughts and emotions affect our actions.

CBT says: Money-related Events 💥 in your past affect your Thoughts 🧠.

Your Thoughts affect your Feelings 🫦. Your Feelings affect your Actions 🎬. Actions gives us Results, aka your current money life 💸.

Let's pretend my current money life is . . . secretly crying over my empty wallet and wondering why I always spend money without thinking. ✨ PRETEND. ✨

What in the cognitive behavioral wizardry might've happened here?

Let's say you watched your mom struggle to make ends meet, work several jobs, and tell you to be grateful for food and a roof over your head. This is the Event. 💥

OUCH. OUCH MY FEELINGS ALREADY

Because of that Event, your Thoughts might be like, "We never have enough money." 🧠 Maybe your Feelings about money throughout your childhood = Frustrated. 🫦

So years later, when you finally earn your own money, all those pent-up frustrated feelings lead to an Action 🎬: You spend it all right away. Your brain is like, "We never had enough and WHO KNOWS WHEN I'LL GET IT AGAIN. AAAAH!"

Result? 🧨 Low checking account. Low self-esteem. Low-key crying in your new Air Force 1s. Rinse and repeat. Financial trauma, baby!

SHANI, STAY OUT OF MY RECEIPTS, PLEASEEEEE!

So, to confirm: I'm not just bad at money. Financial trauma is a real thing?!

Yes, m'aaaaam. Everyone's money trauma is different.

You know how babies learn stuff? Our families model stuff for us, and we copy them. We copy their money habits, too.

If Mom charged everything to the credit cards, that's what we might do, too. 🎬🎬

These money habits start deeeep in our past, and so they're deeeep in our systems. If we really want to master our money, we gotta dig into our past first.

Brb. Gotta FaceTime my mom.

Now, this is what actually made me fall in love with financial education, before all the tips and tricks. When it comes to money, we aren't robots. We won't suddenly start working if someone just punches in the right codes. We can stuff our brains with all the financial books and podcasts in the world, but none of it will ever come close to the impact of uncovering the financial foundations already inside each of us.

Just like my mom's lifelong TV revenge, we've all been carrying our own financial stories around. These old money stories get stored down deep, and they eventually turn into adult-sized money decisions.

And now it's time to dig 'em out, y'all. Grab a pen or fire up those voice notes—we're going brainstorming.

WIDE ANGLE

If we wanna dig into our money stories, we can't just order them up like a bacon-egg-cheese at a bodega. We've gotta zoom out and take in the big picture of our money brains first. I've got a few exercises to get us warmed up before we dive in.

Reminder: This isn't a quiz, and no one has to see these answers but you. You gotta be honest, even if what comes out of you sounds ridonkulous; the first thing that comes to mind is usually the truth.

ZOOM OUT! WE NEED A WIDE SHOT

LEVEL 1: Money. Send Tweet.

We'll start with the word *money*—a small word with potentially big baggage. Set a timer for five minutes, and without thinking too hard, write down or talk out the following:

- What images or pictures come to mind when you see the word *money*? (Objects? People? Emojis, memes, scenes from Netflix shows? List 'em all.)
- What words or phrases come to mind when you see the word *money*? (This changes for me every day. Sometimes it's stuff I feel, like, "Wish I had more." Sometimes it's stuff I heard growing up, like, "Do you have money for that?!")
- Do you notice anything happening in your body when you think of the word *money*? Even the tiniest anything? It might help to close your eyes and scan around with your mind. (The most common mentions I've heard: I didn't realize I was clenching my jaw; I feel unease in my stomach; I feel tense in my shoulders or my back; I feel pressure on my chest.)

LEVEL 2: Finish the Sentence

Now that you're warmed up, let's dig a tad deeper. Write out these prompts, or say 'em out loud, and see where your words take you.

- Money makes me happy when . . .
- Money makes me uncomfortable when . . .
- When someone gives me money, my first thought is . . .
- When I think about spending my money, my first thought is . . .
- Talking about money makes me feel . . .

LEVEL 3: Time to Time Travel

Get in my rocket, y'all—we're going time traveling back to that seven-to-nine age we talked about earlier. Pull up a blanket and take some time with your answers. You could even record yourself on video for this one, or make it a bonding moment with a friend.

Go gently—you might touch on some sensitive stuff—and remember that no matter if what you find makes you happy, surprised, or deeply uncomfortable (mine did!), all of it is valid. And remember: Turn to a professional, like a financial therapist (that's a thing!), for more thorough unpacking. You can find one using resources like the Financial Therapy Association.

♥ Talk about money in your **childhood**. What was the feeling about money in your house growing up? Did the adults talk about it in front of you or with you? Was there ever fighting or tension about money, and when? Were you included in conversations about money?

♥ Talk about the **people who raised you**. Who controlled the money in your house? If you had parents or guardians, did they each treat money differently? What was it like when they needed to spend money? What was it like when they needed to save money, if at all? Who taught them about money?

♥ Talk about money in your **culture, your ethnicity, your religion, your heritage**. How is money treated in your culture? Who gets to hold it or spend it? What is it "okay" to spend on, and what's "not okay"? Were you ever taught that money was connected to evil, to greed, to blessings, or to sin? What messages or rules about money might have you absorbed from your family's culture?

♥ Talk about money and your **friends**, both in the past and now. Do you remember feeling like you had more or less money than your friends or the people you went to school with? How did you find out, and what was that like? Did what your friends (or non-friends!) post on social media make you think about money?

🫀 Talk to me about **privilege**—the money-related benefits you got, or didn't get, because of where and how you were born. What privileges did you have growing up that helped you financially? What put you at a financial disadvantage? How might have your family's money been affected by things outside of your control, like gender discrimination, racial discrimination, neurodivergence, having no inheritances, savings, or "fallback" money, being undocumented, or coming to America as immigrants?

$ TALK MONEY TO ME $
WHAT THE BLEEP IS CAPITALISM?

If there's one word that helped me map out my financial feelings in a big way, it's *ASMR whisper* CAPITALISM. Capitalism affects nearly every damn thing we know about money.

The thing is, capitalism is complicated—economists have written whole books about it. I'm just gonna give you the super-surface-level parts we need to understand. Cool?

The official definition: Capitalism is a system where everything needed to make products—like factories, land,

---

oil, ships—is owned by private individuals and companies, instead of being owned by the government.

Tight. So why the hell does this matter?

In capitalism, all of these individuals and companies are focused on one thing only: Profit. Wealth. Competing to make as much money as humanly possible.

And this type of economic system creates a lot of conflicting truths that affect our lives every damn day.

YAY CAPITALISM	BOO CAPITALISM
Since businesses have to compete for our dollar, they gotta do everything they can to make the cheapest possible product–which means cheaper prices for us consumers...	... but, those in power treat their employees like cogs in a machine–paying them the lowest wages they can get away with and sometimes forcing them to work in dangerous conditions.
All that competition between businesses encourages innovation and progress, which means we get new products all the time–and it rewards both individuals and companies for making it past startup mode...	... but, recent decades have seen a growing, devastating imbalance between the superrich, who hoard their wealth, and the poor working class. Some of those companies monopolize or take over their whole industry, so no other company even has a chance to compete.

Since profits pretty much keep increasing, folks who invest in the stock market (me!) keep seeing gains...

... but, to keep up with all this growth and expansion, we're consuming natural resources at a level that is killing people, destroying the planet, and furthering deadly colonial and imperialist agendas.

But, damn, what if the government controlled everything? Byyye, personal freedoms...

... but, the richer the bosses get, the more power they have and the less power the rest of us have—which is the opposite of equality.

Head spinning? Good, then you're right on track. It's hella complex and goes way deeper than what we can fit in here.

If you're sitting here like, "Berna, I have the answer . . . Eat the Rich," you're not wrong—but it's a bit trickier than that.

Capitalism is a system built for imbalance. It's specifically designed to make certain people rich and others (*cough/scream* marginalized communities) poor. It's a system that forces nearly all of us to exploit others in order to "make it." It's a wack-a$$ cycle.

As we learn how capitalism affects our financial freedom throughout the book, we have to keep asking ourselves: How has capitalism affected our lives—the jobs we work, the wages we're paid, the choices we have to make? How can we work within this system to survive? And how can we reimagine other ways of creating things, sharing resources, and supporting each other?

IT'S NOT YOU, :)
IT'S CAPITALISM

OPEN MIC

Looking to dig even deeper into your family's Money Story? If your family is like mine—and this is super-common in BIPOC and immigrant families—you were taught to never talk directly about money, unless you're tryna get whacked by a slipper/belt/Santo Niño statue.

My tip? Get them in **Storytelling Mode**. Instead of asking them direct "Why?" questions that might put them in defense mode, ask them to share their wisdom or earliest money memories. After that, it's up to you to connect the financial dots in their storytelling.

To show you how it's done, I took a deep breath and tried it with my parents. Lemme pass the mic to the two people who may have shaped my money brain the most.

Q: Do you remember what you did with your very first paycheck?

Mom: I started working in the Philippines, when I was seven or eight. My job was to sell supot, or grocery bags, in our local market. And since part of my job was to help my single mom raise us seven children, every single peso, I gave to Mama—your Lola Magdalena. She would keep our pay and give us only what we needed for school and things. Even when I got older and earned my very first paycheck from the Dole Cannery in Honolulu, that paycheck still went to Mama.

Dad: Yeah, before, one peso was a lot of money. A kid would never hold a peso. When I joined the military after high school, around twenty-five percent of my paycheck automatically went straight to my parents, since I was underage.

Mom: That's how it is when you grow up poor—it didn't ever enter our heads to talk about money or to ask why. It's tradition; it's your responsibility to help out the family.

🎤 Q: What's the first thing you bought yourself with your own money?

Dad: Levi's! I was twelve years old, and, well, they were the most popular jeans. Back in the day, there was no mall—I know we sound ancient—but I bought them from a small store, with the money I made from working in a gas station while growing up in Yigo, Guam.

Mom: When we immigrated from the Philippines to Waipahu, my first adult purchase was new clothes. I always grew up with hand-me-downs, and because Mama was a seamstress, she would revive the hand-me-downs every year on my birthday. But sometimes I would hide the money Mama gave me for school and one day I bought a brand-new halter dress and bell-bottoms. That's probably why once I got my own money, I always bought clothes. Because we never, ever got new clothes.

FOCUS IN

All right—rewind to your answers from page 15. Take in all the different things that make up the beginnings of your Money Story. Did any surprising scenes come up for you?

Cause, listen—when I first dug into my money backstory, I wasn't feeling so superhero; some of what I found made me weep like it was a Pixar movie instead. Some surprising scenes popped into my head that I forgot about.

It was like—*boom*—there I was, passing through our kitchen, seeing all the bills and envelopes spread on the kitchen table, my mom and dad talking low and heavy in Tagalog so we wouldn't understand. (Though you don't need a translator to feel that kind of tension.)

Boom—there I was, peeking through the crack in my mom's bedroom. She'd been lying there in the dark for several days. We'd just found out that the 2008 housing crisis crushed us, and we had to file for bankruptcy.

And now, being able to put all those scenes into focus, I felt something new—something I call financial empathy. I could see how my parents might have felt, trying to keep it all together because they thought it would be healthier for us not to know, not to stress about it.

While I could connect a lot of my current money habits to these moments, I could also see how my Money Story wasn't any one person's "fault." Our Money Stories are made up of many scenes and—hard shoutout to my immigrant parents—everyone is doing the best they can with whatever tools they've got.

Now that the beginning of your Money Story is coming into focus, I want you to be like a creative director and list your major money scenes out. What moments made the biggest impact on your money brain?

I try not to think of our Money Stories as good or bad; most stories are a little bit of both. So, for this brainstorm, I want you to make two lists:

Financial boosts—the things that have helped your money life.

Financial bumps—the things that make your money life more challenging now.

Lemme show you what my lists look like, to start you off.

Financial Boosts 📊

What happened...	That means I learned...
My mom took me to open my first savings and checking accounts at sixteen	How banks and debit cards work
I was born in the US, able-bodied, and learned English as my first language	How to get a job, and how paychecks worked, at a young age

Financial Bumps 📉

What happened...	That means I learned...
My family got caught in the early-2000s housing crisis and filed for bankruptcy, but never talked about it	To be afraid and distrustful but silent about money; that investing ends in disaster
At home, it was all about "that's too expensive," but out to dinner with relatives, everyone fought for the check	That you should spend money to show people you love them, even if you secretly can't afford it

OoooohWHEEEE. See all that?

Look at all the financial ups and downs you've already been through. You've got levels to you, like any movie's hero.[2] Your

---

2 Who saw *Black Panther*? Killmonger made some points about colonization.

Money Story is much deeper than you even knew—and it's just now coming into focus for you, friend.

Maybe we learn not to blame ourselves for the bumps in our financial past. Maybe we understand our financial weak spots better, so we can interrupt harmful habits in the future.

But my greatest hope is that we become more empathetic and forgiving toward ourselves and the money behaviors of those around us—because no one's Money Story is simple.

$ TALK MONEY TO ME $
THE FRUGAL FLEX THEORY

I have a deeply unscientific financial theory about why some of us are confused about money. I call it my Frugal-Flex Theory. It's backed purely by the fact that I've laugh-cried about it with way too many strangers who can relate.

The Frugal-Flex Theory is as follows: Your family ping-ponged between acting hella Frugal or Flexing money they didn't really have.

One day, your household might've sounded like: "You want to go to McDonald's? AYE. We have rice at home." Or, "Oh, your friend can afford the new Jordans? Go live with your friend, then, let them raise you!"

But in the same day, you might go to a family gathering, and suddenly it's like: *wears head-to-toe, definitely fake "designer labels" and loudest possible insignia Louis Vuitton bag to the local all-you-can-eat buffet and fights for the bill.*

... And all that in one day of living in my family.

I know now that my family made major sacrifices as immigrants. They wanted nice things to prove they'd achieved that American dream—that the sacrifice was worth it—even if it put us in debt. But still, as a kid? W H A T. HOW CONFUSING.

Give it a think, discuss this with your group chat, or find me on the Internets and talk money to me: Is the Frugal-Flex Theory a part of your Money Story, too? How might it have affected the way you treat money now?

AAAAND ACTION

We've sketched out your Money Story so far, but spoiler alert: your Money Story has just started. From here on out, you're the director. We can't rewrite the past, but now we can say exactly how we want the rest of the story to go. (And when it doesn't go perfectly? That's part of your story, too.)

And that's exactly what we're gonna do: script the sequel to our Money Stories. Have you ever written something that you never meant to show to anyone, just so you can get all of your feels out? Yup, that's the energy we're bringing to this last prompt. I want you to write a letter to Money.

All you've gotta do is start with "Dear Money," and let your brain flow from there. If you're like, wheh?, here are a few things to keep in mind that might help get the feelings out:

🖎 If Money were a person, what's the first thing you'd say to them? Or whisper to them? Or yell at them? (Sometimes I wish Money had shoulders that I could SHAKE.)

🖎 Look back at what you learned from your Financial Bumps, and ask yourself: Are those "lessons" still true? Are these "lessons" messing with my money life? How do I want to rewrite or change these beliefs for the better?

🖎 How do you want to feel about Money from now on? What do you hope Money does for you? Think about future generations and what you'd like to pass on—what kind of legendary Money Story would you want them to hear?

🖎 Who are you bringing along in your new Money Story? Who do you wish could read this book with you? Whose shoulders are you standing on today, that made it possible for you to even access this book?

< **Notes**

Dear Money,

BOI. 🥶 YOU CONFUSE ME. But it's time for me to take control of this complicated relationship.

I grew up thinking that wanting more of you made me a greedy person. I realized that this belief made me frickin' scared of you, so I never wanted to deal with you.

Y'know what, though? I think you are actually a bada$$ tool that can get me where I want to go.

Friends? 😌

How Do You Want Money to Make You Feel?

If you're feeling stuck, lemme help you out a bit and zoom back in on my mama.

When she decided to fill her whole damn house with TVs one day, it wasn't actually all those TVs she wanted. What she really wanted was her pride back. What she really wanted was to feel powerful, like her neighbor. She never wanted to feel that shame, sadness, or anger ever again; she wanted to feel in control. And she wanted the money to make it happen.

As Shani said, our financial desires are actually driven by our emotions. And we have the power to call those emotions out so that they don't take over our whole financial lives. So, give it a think, and add it to your letter: How do you want Money to make you feel?

When you say . . .	. . . what you might really want:
I want to be rich	I want to feel safe; I want to feel powerful
I want to pay off debt	I want to feel free; I don't want to feel anxious
I want to afford to hang with friends	I want to feel included; I don't want to feel left out
I want to buy a sweet car	I want to feel respected and admired; I don't want to feel ashamed or unworthy
I want to help my family	I want to feel capable, responsible, included, loved; I don't want to feel inept, ungrateful, useless

Let 'er rip. To be honest, Money has probably been running your life—with very little feedback from you—for a long time.

This is your official notice to Money that the power is shifting, and you're about to control the plot from now on. In your letter, let 'em hear you, once and for all.

GREAT WORK, EVERYONE, TAKE 5!

Now, step back. Stretch your neck. Do that motorboat thing with your lips and blow out aaaalllll the financial feels, because, friend, you went deep.

Do you understand how powerful a tool that is? When you know your Money Story, you gain control of your financial future. If you make mistakes, you can look back and go, "Ah, yeah. I've seen this in my Money Story before, and I can try to do things differently now."

When you know your Money Story, you can feel a little more understanding not just for the folks who helped shape your financial life, but for the fantastically complex Main Character that is You. You give yourself permission to celebrate all your financial boosts, and forgive yourself through every financial bump.

All that's left is to make you into the financial hero of your story—the money Main Character you were always meant to be.

(And when your inspiring money-or-otherwise story gets picked up by a major studio someday, you can trust and believe my mom and I will be watching on ALL of her revenge TVs.)

WAIT, WHAT?

It's a lot, right? Brain spinnin', knees weak, arms heavy, Mom's spaghetti?

I gotchu. We'll summarize your homework at the end of each chapter. Remember to take your time, and only move on to the next chapter when you've done the work and feel confident about learning more.

How to start unpacking your financial feels:

$ Grab something to write with or something to record yourself.

$ Warm up with some simple Level 1 and 2 questions on page 15.

$ Start digging into your past Money Story and map out the financial lessons you've learned from those boosts and bumps on page 23.

$ Write out your new Money Story with a letter to Money, starting on page 26.

2

HELLA CONTROL
(AKA BUDGETING)

You know what? I'm proud of you for diving deep into your financial feels. That stuff is heavy.

I'm so proud, I'm gonna just tell you my juiciest financial secret weapon right now.

clears throat The way to achieve your fanciest, wildest, most delicious money dreams—aside from getting fair pay, of course—is by doing a beautiful thing with a fugly name.

Budgeting.

WAIT DON'T CLOSE THE BOOK—

Listen: I KNOW. I didn't choose to give it a name that sounds like something Jabba the Hutt burped out. I can already feel some of y'all tuning me out because you think I'm about to try to make you love spreadsheets.[3]

---

3 The thing is, I love a spreadsheet. But I'm gonna keep that to myself for now.

But somewhere along the way, someone lied to us about budgeting, because it's the first financial habit I learned that truly changed my entire life.

- 🦋 How did I finally figure out exactly why I'm broke and how to fix it? Budgeting.
- 🦋 How was I able to pay off $50,000 of debt and save up to quit my job and travel for a whole freakin' year? . . . A phatter paycheck, and hard work, to be honest, but also? Budgeting.
- 🦋 What makes me feel in control of my money—and therefore my life—every dang day, even when I really am broke? Yup.

That's my favorite part about it: the feeling of control. Before I discovered budgeting, I spent so long feeling like my money was just blowing in and out of my life like a toxic ex. I had no idea budgeting meant being your own financial boss and giving yourself permission to spend money, consciously, even joyfully. Budgeting is about getting to decide what you truly want in life—and then building the simple structure to make that happen.

SING IT WITH ME: BUDGETING

Your honor . . . budgeting is my best freakin' friend.

The actual definition of budgeting is something like, "allocating sums of money for a particular purpose." Literally my eyeballs just dried up with boredom. But I define budgeting totally differently. And I think you'll like my way slightly better.

BUDGETING = YOU ARE THE CEO OF YOUR LIFE

My style of budgeting takes a bit of imagination: we are pretending you are the CEO of a company called Your Life.[4]

The whole company's mission is to make you, the CEO, happy.

Your employees are your dollars.

And all you gotta do is give each dollar a job. (That's literally what budgeting is.)

For now, you've got three different jobs that you can give a dollar: Needs, Wants, and Dreams.

JOB #1: Needs

Before we talk about your future, Present You is first in line—and they've got this pesky thing called, uh, the basic needs. It can be hilariously expensive to be a human person. *coughs in capitalism*

This is where our first money job, your Needs, enters the chat. This is the money you use to buy stuff you literally Need to survive and thrive, like food and shelter. I'm talking about your core adult-mammal, absolutely-need-to-function stuff.

Need Dollars have a huge job, because, hi: we wanna keep you functioning, my friend. Your budget's first priority is to keep you safe, because it's hard to dream in survival mode. Covering your needs first gets your head above water so you can actually think ahead.

---

4 Tiny spoiler alert: YOU ACTUALLY ARE.

This is CEO-you telling some of your dollars: **"Your job is to keep me alive. No pressure."**

JOB #2: Dreams

Important CEO-level question: What is your biggest money dream—the one thing you want your money to do most? Pay off debt? Skydive in Santorini? Have enough saved to someday quit working forever?

Great. That's your company's second goal. And when I say Dreams, what I'm really talking about is (puts mic closer to mouth) saving some money for the future.

The concept of saving money *also* tends to make people's eyeballs dry out, so let's remix your perspective a bit: You're not just "saving money." You're paying yourself. (Hello. CEO.)

NO. You're not just paying yourself. You're paying Future You first.

When you decide to save a dollar instead of spending it, you're scooching yourself toward making your biggest money dreams come true. So when you receive any amount of money, the first thing you can do is grab some of it and say, **"Aye. Your job is to make my future Dreams come true, little dudes,"** and stick those dollars in a safe place for savings.

When you first start budgeting, I truly don't care whether  you're depositing $1 or $100 in your savings. I just care that you deposit *something*, every single time you get money. What matters right now is that you practice saving consistently—like flexing a muscle little by little to build it up, so that saving for your dreams becomes an instinct.

We'll talk more about getting those savings muscles swole in chapter 3, but in short: that's how a savings fund—and therefore, a money dream—truly grows, y'all. Not by putting in "whatever's left" after spending mindlessly (because we all know "whatever" ends up being "lol, nothing"), but by putting away Dream Dollars before you spend on anything extra.

Future You deserves that kind of VIP treatment, don't you think?

JOB #3: Wants

Now here's the fun part. Literally. The third job you can give your dollars is Wants, aka the things you don't need to survive, but they make life delicious.

Imagine you taking some of your dollars and going, **"Your job is just to straight-up keep me happy, smol friends."** Yup, for the folks in the back: I'm telling you that once you've practiced flexing that saving muscle and covered your needs, your next financial priority is Buying Whatever You Want Because You Deserve to Enjoy Your Money.

To me, the whole point of budgeting isn't just to organize your

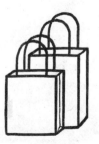
money and pay bills. It's to cover your bases so you know exactly how *much* money you can have freakin' fun with. And putting away my Want Dollars is like giving myself a Have Freakin' Fun allowance, so I always know exactly how much I can make it rain ON. MY. SELF.

Do I Need It Or Do I Want It?

When you start figuring out what your Wants and Needs are, your brain is probably gonna start arguing with itself. I need to eat, so this takeout pizza is a Need, right? This deep, guttural urge to scream at my Fave Artist at a concert—is that a Need, too?

It can get a little confusing, so let's clarify a few things here.

NEEDS	WANTS
Food you eat every day, like groceries and daily meals	Not-super-necessary food, like eating out at restaurants, takeout, extra snacks; anything that would make my mom go "AYE, WE HAVE RICE AT HOME."
Housing, like paying rent, or covering your families' housing needs	Extra beauty, fashion, or clothing expenses
Transportation to get your booty to school, work, and back home	Vacation, road trips, outings with friends
Health needs, like medicine or services to keep you feeling safe and keep your body and brain in shape	Hobbies, like games, sports, clubs, and memberships
House bills that keep your life running, like paying a phone bill, internet, or minimum payments on things like credit cards	Entertainment subscriptions, like your TV streaming stuff, your music streaming stuff, your erry-month self-care services

We gotta be honest with ourselves when deciding what's a Want vs. a Need—but sometimes, life isn't so budget-binary, and that is totally okay. For example, if you're sending money to support family abroad, I wouldn't stress over the category. What matters is that you give things like Family Money a specific space in your budget and not just "whatever's left" so you can consistently cover what's important without neglecting yourself.

Everyone's Needs and Wants are different, and it's a no-judgment zone here—but keep in mind that spending too much on Wants and not enough on your Needs is a one-way ticket to Broke City in Stressville, USA.

'Kay. I Got Money. How's This Work?

Let's say your grandma does that hilarious thing where she calls you to the corner of the room and quietly slides you a $50 bill so your mom won't see. Love that for you.

Put that CEO hat/fedora/flower crown on, because it's time to give each of those 50 dollars a job: Needs, Wants, or Dreams? You have some choices to make.

- 💰 You might decide to save all $50 for your Dreams, since you've had your eye on a specific sweater you saw on the internets and have no immediate plans for Wants this week. BOOM. BUDGETING.

- 💰 You might decide to stick $25 in a Dream Sweater envelope at home, and then stick the other $25 in your wallet for Wants because you and your friends have a weekly boba and popcorn chicken addiction. BOOM. BUDGETING.

- 💰 You might only stick $10 in your Dream Sweater savings

account, because you actually really Need $40 to pay dues to your intramural cornhole league this month. BOOM. BUDGETING.

As long as every last dollar has a job, your job here is done. BOOM. YOU'RE BUDGETING. I COULD WEEP.

Now, to make sure your dollars are doing their best, you gotta give them room to work. You know how the different departments of a company often work on separate floors or in separate buildings? Your Need, Want, and Dream Dollars should all live in their own separate spots—whether that's separate cash envelopes or separate bank accounts. (We'll get more into those account options in the next chapter.)

This takes all the guessing out of spending your money—you'll always know exactly how much you have to spend, depending on the item. You can literally look at your Dream Dollars to see if you can *afford* that Internet Sweater. And you'll be less likely to accidentally spend your rent money (Need!) on brown sugar boba (Want!).

Later on, you can create as many "jobs" as your life needs, still giving each "job" its own account or spot. Totally up to you; it's your company, boo.

BUILD A BUDGET:
HOW MUCH DOES A MONTH OF MY LIFE COST?

Listen: no company can function just by crossing their fingers and hoping there's enough money. A smart CEO takes a look at the past, builds a plan from there, but stays flexible about the future.

And that's just what a budget is: your plan for your future dollars.

So, here are your first few action items: just like real CEOs have to try to figure out how much it might cost to start their company, we're gonna see how much your life costs over one month. It's about to get all math-experiment-y up in here.

1. Grab a comfy seat, a calculator, and something to write on. Split the page into two lists: Needs and Wants. (Or Life and Fun. Or Adulting and Ratchetry. Get wild!)

2. Pull up the receipts from your spending in the last four weeks. You might download your last month's bank statements or credit card transactions; you might just need to consult your Google Calendar, your Venmo, and your brain to piece it together.

3. Take each purchase you've made and write it under either your Needs or Wants list, like so:

MY NEEDS	MY WANTS
1-month bus pass ($60)	Streaming/binging service ($14)
Contact lenses ($20)	Rideshare to mall ($11)
Phone bill ($40)	Pizza with volleyball team ($7)
Volleyball team monthly dues ($15)	Shirts from Labor Day sale ($22)
Dreams deposit–Summer in Vegas ($30)	Paid Ollie for movie tickets ($19)
NEEDS TOTAL: $165	**WANTS TOTAL: $73**

DELISH.

Now, pay close attention—you saw how I fit in a lil' Dream Dollar deposit under Needs? That's because I want you to practice treating your savings as seriously as a bill. Way more on this in chapter 3.

4. Take a deep breath and add up everything in each column, so you get a total cost for Needs and a total cost for Wants.

5. Do a little shoulder shimmy, because this is A Moment: you've arrived at the two numbers that will help your money life more than any other:

> Your Monthly Needs (**$165 in Example Land**) and
> and your Monthly Wants (**$73 in Example Land**).

Now of course, you won't always spend the same amount every month, but what matters is you've got this lil' bit of real-life data to start working with. If you add those two numbers up, you can see a rough estimate of your Entire Life Bill for a whole month—and then you can use that number as a flexible base to plan for next month.

For instance, in Example Land:

$165 for Needs + $73 for Wants =
My Entire Life Bill costs about ($238) a month.

So now you might say: $238 is your monthly budget. Now you know you need to earn at least $238 each month, so that you can comfortably cover your budget and afford your Wants and Needs.

This is a huge deal, because when you know your Entire Life Bill, you can always figure out the answer to the all-important life question:

WITH MY BUDGET I AM UNSTOPPABLE

WHY AM I ALWAYS BROKE??

Do you have or earn enough money each
month to pay your Entire Life Bill?

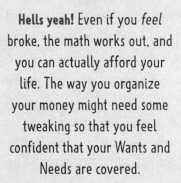

Yup!

Hells yeah! Even if you *feel* broke, the math works out, and you can actually afford your life. The way you organize your money might need some tweaking so that you feel confident that your Wants and Needs are covered.

What do I do? Double-check your Wants and Needs lists to make sure that's how you wanna be spending your money next month. What part of your life feels like it needs more dollars? How can you move things around, or plan to earn more, to make you feel more secure?

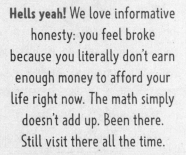

Nope!

Hells yeah! We love informative honesty: you feel broke because you literally don't earn enough money to afford your life right now. The math simply doesn't add up. Been there. Still visit there all the time.

What do I do? There's no magical budgeting trick to this: you either need to snip expenses, earn more, or both—whatever gets you to cover your Entire Life Bill.

And here's the thing: your Life Bill is not a fixed forever-number. Someone's always having a birthday or a baby; some months are just hella more expensive than others. Your budget is meant to bend and snap according to however your life moves.

So instead of hating on yourself with "Dammit, why couldn't I stick to my budget?" Drop that negative energy and ask some curious questions.

🧠 Am I earning enough to afford my actual life?

🧠 How can my budget be more flexible to fit my life?

🧠 What expenses are coming up next month, and how can I remix my current budget to feel prepared?

Sometimes I gotta say no to some of my Wants for the month, because I Need to cover a surprise medical bill. Sometimes I choose to keep my Needs slim—aka I sure *do* have rice at home—so I can afford that Want-y concert ticket I've been manifesting for, like, three years.

Everyone's Needs, Wants, and Dreams are different, and so everyone's choices are different. But the point is, dear CEO: a budget means You've. Got. Choices. They're in your hands. You're the boss.

HOW MUCH AM I *SUPPOSED* TO SPEND EACH MONTH?

Even when I calculated my own Life Bill and came up with my first budget, I still wanted to peek at someone else's paper to know if I was doing it right. Were other people's budgets like mine? Were my Wants way outta whack? Was I saving "enough" for my Dreams?

That's when I stumbled upon Ye Olde 50/30/20 Rule, which has been repeated by financial experts for decades now. This rule says:

$ You "should" spend 50% of your paycheck on your Needs— rent, utilities, gas, phone, all that.

$ You "should" spend 30% of your paycheck on Wants— entertainment, eating out, and all nonessential purchases.

$ And finally, you "should" spend that last 20% of your paycheck on your financial goals—putting money toward your savings, your debt, or any other money Dreams you've got.

Did you feel my aggressive air quotes? That's because that old-school budgeting advice might tell you that if you can't fit your Needs into those fixed percentages, then you're somehow "bad" at money.

But let's cut to the facts of Present Day:

$ The national cost of living—aka how much it costs to afford your Needs, on average—has risen, but national minimum wage? SHE HAS NOT.

$ The wealth gaps between our richest citizens and our poorest citizens have exploded—so more people are either getting superrich or slipping into poverty, and there are fewer folks living in the "comfortable" middle.

$ Our most marginalized communities—women, people of color, undocumented workers, disabled workers—still earn way less on average than their white, male, cisgender counterparts for the same dang jobs.

$ Living in major cities—aka cities that often offer the most job opportunities—is getting increasingly expensive, making it nearly friggin' impossible to live by the 50/30/20 rule! *breathes into a paper bag*

So, no. We can create the rules that work for us. Here's how I did it:

- 🪙 I tried out the 50/30/20 rule for approximately one paycheck and LOL'd immediately. I was like, "Needs at 50%? In this economy?!"
- 🪙 I tweaked and twerked the numbers for the next few paychecks before I landed at a formula that worked for me, for now: 65% for Needs, 25% for Wants, 10% for Dreams.
- 🪙 I realized that I really wanted to build an Emergency Savings as quickly as possible. I made some massive life changes, chopped a ton of expenses, and for a few months, I lived off this formula: 30% for Needs (so . . . roommates), 7% for Wants (it . . . was a rough year), and 63% went straight to Dream savings.

That's the beautiful thing about budgeting: every new paycheck or chunk of money is like hitting a big ol' RESET button on your company rules. You can throw out what didn't work and change your budget according to what's coming up. As long as you always have Dreams, Needs, *and* Wants built into your budget, you make your own rules as you go. As the CEO, you've got power like that.

OPEN MIC

So now you get the concept of a budget—but where are you supposed to *do* your budget?

I don't know about you, but I learn best when someone gives me real-life examples. For that, I turn to my people. Lemme pass the mic to some folks in my @heyberna online community who make my financial life so much spicier.

I asked my Money Friends: What do you use to budget? Literally, where does your budget live?

🎙 "In a paper bullet journal—I have a spending tracker next to a bar chart with updates of my savings goals." —ChiChai M.

🎙 "I pull cash out when I need to save and put it in envelopes based on priority." —Deven Z.

🎙 "When I first started, it was on a Post-it note in my wallet so I could track EVERYTHING throughout my day." —Khalisa G.

🎙 "Google Sheets—I track income, needs, and savings, and then the rest of my money I can spend on whatever." —Mylee E.

🎙 "I use an app that connects to my bank and makes tracking easy. Had to try a few though before I found one that works!" —Allison M.

🎙 "Pen and paper, baby! I like doing my math by hand and being able to see my edits as I go." —Jess D.

BUDGETING, BUT MAKE IT FUN

I'm psyched for your new budgeting journey . . . but I know how it goes. You'll get super hyped about this new money plan, but then life happens, and you might fall off for a week. And then a month. And then like a deflated birthday balloon, the hype feelings disappear, replaced by their Fugly Cousins: Shame, Guilt, and Failure.

Honestly, budgeting often means taking an ice-cold honest look at the financial reality of your life, and that can be a ton of emotional work. It's not that you're bad at budgeting. But it might be that budgeting stresses you out or straight-up bores you. Fair!

Luckily, budgeting-but-make-it-fun is my specialty. And I don't mean "throw a pizza party for your disgruntled, underpaid employees" fake fun. As CEO of my own life, I've found ways to legitimately fall in Serious Like with budgeting—here's how.

Meet With Your CFO

The CEO of any major company does not have time to worry about money every single day. That's why they hire a CFO—a chief financial officer—and have regular meetings to bang out the money stuff together. That's what I want you to do. (Hint: You're the CFO, too.)

I'm saying: put actual time on your calendar, at least an hour once every week or every two weeks, to do all your money stuff at once—like an ongoing money date with yourself. I actually call my money date my BAE Day. Yes, because I feel like my budget is my boo, but also? Once I get paid, I budget my paycheck Before Anything Else. (Eh?!)

If you have a job and your payday is, say, every other Friday? Have your CFO meetings every other Friday, so that you can organize your money as soon as you get it. Like, before you accidentally trip on a Friday night and spend your whole paycheck on happy hour hot wings. (Don't you hate when that happens?)

This is the moment you actually put all those Need, Want, and Dream Dollars to work. You might spend this hour:

$ Opening up your bank accounts and making sure nothing weird is happening.

$ Moving your money around to cover your Needs, Wants, and Dreams for the next two weeks—either 50/30/20 style, or according to whatever rules you chose.

$ Peeking at your savings goals and seeing your progress.

$ Asking yourself, either out loud or journal-style:

-How have I spent my money during the last two weeks? How do I feel about it now?

-What would I change if I could go back?

-What can I do different or plan for in the next two weeks?

One of the reasons I love a CFO moment? Multiple times a week, my brain is like: "Ugh, all these random money tasks, things to do, questions to Google—when am I gonna get my financial shiz together?!" Instead of stressing about it in the moment, I keep a lil' list on my phone where I dump all my money worries that come up during the week. It's kind of like keeping an agenda for my CFO meeting, which makes me less anxious because I know I have a designated time to get it to it later.

The more consistent you are with your BAE Day (or whatever delightful name you call it), the less you'll have to worry about your money during allll your other life hours. You'll know your CFO (aka you) has got your back.

Choose Your Fighter

When I first approached the Googles and asked, "plz, sir, what is . . . budget?" a ton of articles and podcasts suggested using certain apps, downloadable spreadsheets, or intense-looking programs. If that makes you want to hurl, no worries: you are allowed to choose the budgeting weapon that best suits you. And if you can't find it, you can totally make one up. That's what I did.

For me, the answer was journaling. I've journaled nearly every night since I was eight, so I decided to open up a Google Doc and start a money journal.

And every other Wednesday afternoon—my biweekly CFO meeting—not only did I move my money around for my Needs, Wants, and Dreams, but I wrote out my thoughts about it all, too. I wrote about how I spent my last paycheck: Did I have any regrets? What worked, what didn't, what budgeting rules do I need to tweak for next time? And I wrote about my *next* paycheck: What's coming up that I need to prepare for now?

Slowly but surely, a friggin' miracle happened: the more I started to journal about my money thoughts, the more I saw patterns in my spending. For example, I saw that even though I'm a frugal cheap-o with myself, I spend mindlessly when I'm treating my friends and family. I decided to challenge myself with a Treat Your Loved Ones allowance—$50 every two weeks, to start—and see how far it would go between now and my next CFO moment.

While I was beating myself up about not using the "right" budgeting tools, I was tracking my experiences with money in my journal—not realizing that that 👏 is 👏 budgeting.👏 I loved budgeting even more because I created a unique system for myself.

Shall we brainstorm what money system might work for you?

Maybe I'm More Manual

If you love details and getting your hands in the weeds (it me!), you might be more into manual budgeting. You could free-write in a journal, or try out any number of actual, published budget journals out there. You can keep track of your Life Bill in that journal, track what you spend, and whip open that journal during your CFO moment.

If you're mostly dealing with cash, or you're really looking to limit yourself and not risk overspending on debit or credit cards, you can try out a cash envelope system. This means you're doing all or most of your spending in cash. You'll grab all your cash, label a few paper envelopes with each of your budget categories—Needs, Wants, Dreams, whatever you like—and manually stick your cash in each envelope.

You might head to the grocery store and challenge yourself to only spend what's in the Grocery envelope, or stick your Eating Out with Friends envelope in your bag before a night out. It's manual financial discipline on a whole new level.

Maybe I'm a Tech Head

There are endless amounts of new financial technology, or fintech, flooding the Interwebs every day, and hallelujah for that. You can find apps that will connect to your bank account, track your spending for you, or create an entire digital budget according to your life.

You might try searching:

$ Best Free Budgeting apps

$ Top Budgeting Tools [insert year]

$ Free Budgeting Spreadsheets

Fintech moves so fast, there are new budgeting apps being launched . . . by the time I finish typing this sentence. Feel free to take your time, test out different approaches, and shop around to see what products feel best for you.

Whether you're more manual, more techie, a mix of both, or your own category entirely, there is no *right* way to track your budget. Your budgeting method is specific to you, just like your budget itself, and just like your life. The more personalized your approach is, the more you'll be excited to take ownership of how your money moves.

It may change according to your mood, your life season, your financial situation, but the important thing is to mold your budgeting method to you, no matter the medium.[5]

---

5 Honestly, all I want to hear is that someone came up with Budgeting Zumba one day. Can someone text me when that happens?

Make the Bots Do the Bill-Paying Work

Here at the HeyBerna School of Budgeting (I just decided that that's a thing), we pride ourselves on one thing: laziness. I mean, efficiency. That's why I'd like to introduce you to my friend: Automated Payments. Automated Payments is a fancy term for "when my bills get paid without me doing a thing besides tapping a few buttons."

It's super common for any gimme-your-money company (utilities, cell phone bill, loans, etc.) to offer Automated Payments. You connect a bank account to the company's website, and they'll automatically take money from your account and pay your bill on the same day each month. All you gotta do is make sure there's enough funds in there to cover it before the bill is due. (Which you can do during your CFO meeting, of course.)

An even bigger boss move? If you're employed, make your real-life boss budget for you. Some employers can split up your paycheck and stick certain amounts of your money in several different accounts *for* you, if you ask. For example, you could ask them to stick 50% of your paycheck in your Needs account, 30% in your Wants account, and 20% in your Dreams account. Boom: budgeting without lifting a finger. Most Efficient CEO of the Year award GOES TO YOU.

Trick Your Budget Brain

Now, here's the true trick to keeping your CFO meeting: think of the funnest, most self-care-y rituals that you never have time for. Do you wish there was more room in your life for a weekly charcoal mask or a pantsless bardcore dance party? Do you brain-complain about never finding time to binge-watch a certain show?

Here's your chance. Make absolutely sure you're doing That Thing before, during, or after your budgeting sesh.

It's called habit stacking: a concept made popular by best-selling author and brain-hacker J. S. Scott. If you're trying to learn a new habit, you've got to sandwich the new habit between old things you already love to do.

I know a person who always does a full face of makeup and puts on her cutest outfit before her CFO meeting. She would send me a selfie before every budgeting sesh.

I know another fantastic human who always puts on an all-money-song playlist and gets up to dance after every deposit. They make sure to surround themselves with their favorite snack—roasted seaweed—as they budget, and always have *The Office* playing in the background. They said RITUAL.

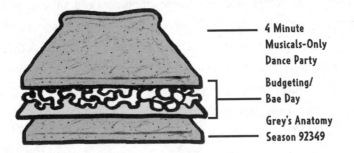

4 Minute
Musicals-Only
Dance Party

Budgeting/
Bae Day

Grey's Anatomy
Season 92349

Both clients hardly ever missed their CFO meetings. Why? Because habit stacking makes their brains go: "Oh, budgeting means also doing (insert other awesome thing I love)? THEN I. LOVE. BUDGETING."

Even if you don't love budgeting right away, you'll start to look forward to this time as a form of self-care. And let me remind you, if no one's told you yet today:

MONEY CARE IS SELF-CARE

Gather Your Peoples

As the world's dopest CEO/CFO, you're almost set: you've got your Life Bill, you've got your CFO meeting, you've got a few tricks to personalize the whole shebang. You're just missing one thing: Money Friends. You didn't think I'd let you keep the delicious joy of budgeting all to yourself, did you?

You need folks to bring along on your budgeting journey—humans with whom you feel safe sharing, venting, and most important, celebrating. Ideal Money Friends will be encouraging, but hold you accountable—meaning, they won't be afraid to tell you, "Aye. Did you do your budgeting this month? Get your schnit together. What do you want more: the newest Nike drop or your lifelong dream of sleeping in an elephant sanctuary?"

Remember: chances are, your ancestors did everything in community—especially for us BIPOC folk.[6] Community is especially clutch with supposedly-taboo things like money, where, historically, those in power have kept us quiet, uneducated, and isolated on purpose. Finding good Money Friends is honestly a low-key form of political resistance.

Your lucky Money Friends should be:

$ People with similar financial goals and values as

---

6 Tbh, I don't know if the hyper-American concept of Do Everything On Your Own is working all that well for us. . . . No, wait, I do know. It sucks.

yours—maybe you're both working students trying to reach a savings goal around the same time.

$ People who aren't suuuper close to you. (I know, I know. Think twice about your besties; they're often too likely to tell you to treat yourself when you're tryna stay focused.)

You can do your CFO meeting/budgeting sessions together—that way, you've got someone to rant with, ask questions, or just body roll with about your budgeting wins. They can also simply be someone you text when you need "Okay, foreal, do I Want this or do I Need this?"-type feedback.

And of course, use the internet—hop into any of the finance communities on your favorite social platforms. Just be careful to not share any personal, trackable information; the internet is where the trolls live, too.

I'll be yakking about more Money Friends ideas throughout this whole book, but for now, tattoo it on your financial heart: You do not. Have to do this. ALONE.

Celebrate Your Wins

Last, but absolutely not least:

You have to celebrate your money wins. It's mandatory. Company policy. CEO said so. Why? Because FUN. And celebrating your money wins just makes you wanna win even more.

Usually, when you do something like pay a bill, that Submit Payment moment is completely anticlimactic. All that labor, all that money, and all you get is a couple of silent screen taps and a stale confirmation email?! SCAM.

Until technology catches up to us and spews confetti out of the screen anytime we hit a financial milestone, we've got to be each other's financial cheerleaders.

When I first started that Money Journal Google Doc, it was a totally solo endeavor—I didn't tell anyone about it because, of course, I thought we're "supposed" to keep money stuff to ourselves. But then I thought: "Screw it. I'm proud of this funky money thing I came up with, and I'm gonna share it because I feel like it." I posted a quick video on my socials of me scrolling through that Google Doc and added a caption explaining how my weird system actually made me excited to budget for the first time ever.

And the notifications. Went. WILD.

I was blown away at the reactions I received, especially from other women of color. But the best part? I received message after message of people saying things like, "I've never seen anyone like me talk about their money before. I didn't know we could do that—thank  you," or, "Seeing this post made me actually consider getting my money life together."

The simple act of sharing my money win not only made me more excited to keep going—it also opened up the conversation of money for folks all around me. Celebrating my money win out loud enabled others to see themselves winning, too.

I'll be honest: Due to my complicated relationship with capitalism, I don't necessarily want to be an actual CEO of any big ol' company. That's why budgeting is sort of a fun cosplay for me, because I can set one simple rule that most CEOs can't: if I'm not generally having fun, I don't want it.

Budgeting is my financial activism in action; it's my way of taking back the shame and powerlessness I've always felt with money. To control my money in such a chaotic world feels empowering, but to enjoy it? To personalize my money process, to literally giggle and dance as I budget, and to connect with others over money the way we never have before? That feels revolutionary.

Every deposit, submitted to the tune of a Megan Thee Stallion money song, brings a flavor of fun to my life that I didn't know could exist. Every dollar dedicated to my Needs, Wants, or Dreams feels like a baby step toward financial empowerment that could last generations.

I finally feel some control over my financial future. I get to make choices so that my money takes care of *me*. And I get to shake a little somethin' while I do it.

WAIT, WHAT?

Budgeting is a multi-step dance, friends, so it's important to go slow and give yourself a few months—months, I said!—to practice, try, freak out, remix your steps, and try again.

How to start building your budget:

$ Take a look at what you spent last month, divide those expenses into Wants and Needs, and add 'em up to get your Entire Life Bill page 38.

$ Peek at the 50/30/20 rule on page 42 and decide on a percentage split to try on your next paycheck.

$ Choose the budgeting method starting on page 48 that straight-up sounds the most fun for you.

$ Pick one hour every one or two weeks to have your CFO meeting (page 46), and choose a few methods to make it interesting from page 51.

$ Text one potential Money Friend about your new budgeting plans right now. Like, right-right now.

TAX PARTY

I got one word that gets the financial party going every time. Ready?

TAXES. *foghorn noises, neon lights*

I have to be extra-hype about taxes, y'all: they're such a significant part of Financial Adulting, but typically, nobody tells you how, where, or why we do them. I mean, it's not like there are serious frickin' consequences if you mess up or avoid them. (There are. There really are.)

While this is by no means a complete guide on taxes, I put together a quick little starter guide to get us caught up.

TAXES? DON'T KNOW HER.

Here's a fact that sounds like a joke: the US tax code, which is basically a government document detailing all of our tax rules, is over 75,000 pages long. That's around eighteen times longer than the entire Harry Potter series, and it changes every year.

You can see why taxes are the kind of thing I usually leave entirely up to the experts. That's why I'm passing the mic to my friend Carter Cofield, CPA (Certified Public Accountant), first-gen college grad and tax expert who speaks fluent Tax-ese.

TEXTSPERT

CARTER COFiELD:

- HE/HiM
- CERTiFiED PUBLIC ACCOUNTANT AND TAX EXPERT
- FiRST-GENERATiON COLLEGE GRADUATE
- HELPS ENTREPRENEURS LiVE TAX-FREE

> Carter, ahem—how do I ask a CPA this without feeling hella dumb . . .

> TAXES. WHAT. ALSO, WHY?!

> LOVE these questions. 😬

> Taxes are basically a way for the government to collect money from us regular citizens, so they can pay for stuff we all share.

> Taxes help pay for stuff like public safety, public schools, fixing roads, social services like SNAP food programs, the military, things like that. 🏫 🛣 🗳 🥫

Hm. Okay. I do love a good social service.

But I didn't realize that if we work, our employer often takes taxes out of our paycheck. AUTOMATICALLY.

Like, I was already paying taxes without realizing? Is that not shady as hell?! 😳

I KNOW. It didn't always used to be that way.

See, back in the day—I'm talking like 1913, when income taxes were first implemented in the US—the government used to tally up everyone's tax bill and tell you what you owed at the end of the year. 📋

Can you guess why they stopped doing that??

The government didn't have calculators on their phones?

Oh, and people probably couldn't afford to pay a phat tax bill at the end of the year?

Exactly. People weren't saving for their tax bill, so they wouldn't pay it.

To fix that, the government 🔀 switched it up 🔀 and started taking it out of everyone's paychecks.

That way, the government makes sure they get their money first, before you even see it go.

(But if you're self-employed, you still gotta pay taxes on your own. It's a whole thing.)

🙂 Dang. So it's like . . . instead of everyone Venmo-ing the one person who organized the house party, the person who paid is like, "It's cool, I already talked to all your bosses and took, like, 30% out of all of your paychecks! 🙃🙃"

Yyyyyyup. 👍

Ever wonder who's paying for the stuff around you like public roads and public schools?

If you pay taxes: YOU ARE.

. . . 🙂🙃🙂🙃🙂🙃

HOW DO TAXES WORK?

I see it like this: the Internal Revenue Service (IRS), our government's tax collection agency, is responsible for throwing a never-ending house party called Our Lives. As Carter said, they pay for all these services we see and use every single day.

But once a year—aka tax season, typically from January to April—the IRS pulls up receipts, sees how much it cost them to throw this party, and calculates how much we each owe, depending on how much we each earn.

Then the IRS tells each of us:

$ You didn't pay enough of your share yet; you owe us money (so you gotta **pay taxes**), OR

$ You actually overpaid, so here's some money back (so you get a **tax refund**).

If you're employed, you might see all kinds of taxes being taken out of your paycheck, like:

$ **Federal Income Tax:** Money we pay the US government to run stuff

$ **State Income Tax:** Money we pay our state's government to run stuff

$ **Social Security and Medicare Taxes:** Money we all put in a fund that supports older, retired, and disabled folks. (It's like pooling our money together to care for other people. The idea is that one day, when you need it, you will receive Social Security money, too.)

You might see two other tax-related words on your paycheck:

$ **Gross Income**[7]: How much money you technically earned before they took things out of your paycheck—like taxes, but also company benefits like health insurance and retirement. (More on that later!)

---

7 A good way to remember: It's called gross income because I get a gross feeling in my stomach wishing I could take all that money home. LOLCRY.

$ Net Income: How much money you actually ended up taking home *after* they took all those things out.

When you start to look beyond your paycheck, you'll notice that they've basically found a way to slap taxes on almost everything. Here are a few other taxes you might see in your world:

Sales Tax—that lil' percent you'll see on your receipt when you buy things from a store. This varies from state to state, but basically, it's like the state government charging a lil' fee on top of everything you buy.

Property Tax—just like sales tax, but for homeowners. Property tax is like the state government charging a lil' fee on top of your monthly mortgage payment, aka house payment.

SO . . . DO I HAVE TO PAY TAXES?

This is why taxes get sticky—everyone's financial situation is different. Even if I was qualified to give tax advice, I'd have to know your exact income, your family structure, your documentation status, the rules of the state you live in . . . *sweats in gratitude for actual accountants.* But we can run through some basics so you know what to expect.

You likely do have to pay taxes if:

$ You're earning an income from an employer and they take taxes out of your paycheck. You might qualify for a refund (yay, money!), but do still need to file your taxes to receive it. This changes every year, but in 2021, if you earned over $12,550 from an official employer, you likely had to pay taxes.

$ You are working for someone who reports your pay on their taxes and you earn more than $400 a year—yup, that includes side hustles and summer jobs. You are technically considered an "independent contractor" by the IRS, and you likely need to file taxes to pay self-employment taxes, no matter how old you are.

HOW DO I ACTUALLY DO MY TAXES?

NOT. ALONE.

Please, as your money auntie, I beg you: do not blindly click through an online tax-filing thing and hope for the best. (I did this. I got something wrong and the IRS was not happy.) Do not fudge your financial relationship with the freaking government, lest you get hit by random penalties you didn't know about. You definitely deserve more financial peace of mind than that.

The thing is, How You File Taxes is—sing it again!—different for everyone. Depending on your employment status and other factors, you might be able to file your taxes entirely online, through a free service, like the stuff we mention below. You might have to actually sit down and hand copies of your paychecks and other info to a tax professional so they can do the thing for you.

Get a professional to suggest the right path for you. You're looking for a Certified Public Accountant (CPA), an Enrolled Agent licensed by the IRS, or a licensed attorney. *Not* someone's unqualified, hotbreath uncle.

You can absolutely get free professional help with your taxes, especially if you're doing them for the first time and you've got hella questions. But keep an eye out—lots of low-key predatory financial services might try to charge you for what should be a free service. The tax-help landscape changes every year, but some things to look out for:

$ IRS.gov: Yup, the grabbers themselves are tryna help! Historically, the IRS has offered an online platform called Free File—a hub of resources that tells you who can file their taxes for free, what you'll need for it, and IRS-approved partners to actually file your taxes.

$ Financial Services Around You: Did you know that local libraries, colleges, and community centers often offer free tax preparation services? An organization near you might have a team of IRS-certified volunteers ready to help you for $Free.99. Financial services you might already use, like CreditKarma, also offer free tax-filing resources.

And last but not least, the best resource of them all? Your. Community.

One of the best decisions I ever made was to throw a Tax Brunch. I invited all my fellow money-anxious friends to my apartment, provided snax and dranx, and we all whipped out our laptops and searched for legit tax resources and/or screamed our confusion together.

Some of us learned that we could do our taxes on our own through a free service, and we talked each other through it; some of us worked on finding the right accountant, financial advisor, or service to help. We all walked away feeling way more prepared and less alone.

Whether you recruit your community or a professional, it is crucial to let the right resources in on your tax party. Even if it's a bit soul-sucky, it feels a little less so when you've got the right support.

3

HELLA OPTIONS
(AKA BANK ACCOUNTS)

I had no choice. I had to eat the Shame Crackers.

Time travel with me while I explain, friends. I was twenty-one years old, a wide-eyed and bushy-haired intern at *Glamour* magazine in New York City. (Remember magazines?) I was wandering Bryant Park at lunchtime on a Thursday—so eager, so ambitious, so hungry. Literally. My stomach was anger-crumping for tacos.

Unfortunately, I had been getting emails like these for weeks:

BOFA Bank of America Alert: Courtesy Balance Notification - To ensure delivery, add onlineb

BOFA Bank of America Alert: Account Has Insufficient Funds - Overdraft Protection Applied

BOFA Bank of America Alert: Account Has Insufficient Funds - Overdraft Protection Applied

BOFA Bank of America Alert: Account Has Insufficient Funds - Overdraft Protection Applied

BOFA Bank of America Alert: Courtesy Balance Notification - To ensure delivery, add onlineb

BOFA Bank of America Alert: Courtesy Balance Notification - To ensure delivery, add onlineb

BOFA Bank of America Alert: Account Has Insufficient Funds - Overdraft Protection Applied

Which I was avoiding like the plague, because each one contained some very personal attacks, like:

To: **BERNADETTE ANAT**

Account: **PERSONAL CHECKING/SAVINGS ACCOUNT ending in 9999**

Date: **10/26/2012**

You are receiving this notification to help you manage your account balance.

Your Available Balance fell below $25 to -$199.12 on 10/26/2012 at 5:55 AM ET.*

If your account is overdrawn, fees and/or declined transactions can occur. Consider depositing or transferring money into this account, and signing up for Overdraft Protection if not already enrolled.

Yup. That's a negative sign. I owed my bank money.

When I first saw that my bank account was at -$199.12—ON MY BIRTHDAY, BY THE WAY, IT'S FINE—I thought I was hallucinating. Because the logic of threatening me with a fee seemed effed. The whole reason I went under $0 is because I was Broke-ity McBroke. So the bank would punish me by . . . making me more broke?

Then boom, the embarrassment—it whacked me like a memory foam pillow. It felt like my fault for not keeping track of my expenses, like maybe other adults did. (Probably? No one talked about it, so I assumed everyone else had it on lock.) It felt like my fault for not knowing how banks worked. And as a child of Asian immigrants, raised to strive for perfection in every possible way, this shame and punishment felt sickly familiar. I felt like I deserved it.

But I felt helpless, too. That fee hit me days before my next paycheck, and I had rent to pay, groceries to buy, student loan payments to ignore. Now every purchase, no matter how small, would cost me another $35 in overdraft fees, too. But what else could I do?

At that moment, stomach yodeling while I was staring at my bank account app in Bryant Park, the only lunch option I could afford from the random change at the bottom of my bag were the clearly expired crackers at a nearby coffee cart. The perfect pathetic-ness was almost poetic.

So I sat, I ate the Shame Crackers, and I cried. Then I wiped up my Duane Reade mascara and went back to work. What other choice did I have?

Helplessness is not my favorite feeling—especially when I prided myself on doing my research for everything else in life. Whenever I wanted to buy something, I'd watch every YouTube review, comb through every Reddit thread, and was always Googling "[insert company name] scam???" Why wasn't I doing the same for the company that literally holds my money?

Because I thought banks automatically held the power. I didn't know I could hold my banks to a higher standard. I didn't think to do my freakin' research.

I would've found out that a third of all bank accounts go into the negative each year. I would've found out that banks collect over $12.4 billion in overdraft fees from us each year, too. (Sing it again: billion.) I would've found out that banks clearly benefit off of our mistakes, our broke-ness, and our lack of (access to) knowledge.

At the end of the day, a bank is just like any other company—except they want to hold your money *and* make money off of you at the same time. In a way, choosing a bank is one of the most empowering money decisions you could ever make, because it's honestly an honor for them to hold your hard-earned dollars. The right bank can:

$ Help you feel organized: the ability to divide your money into different digital buckets is a financial game changer.

$ Help you feel safe: you can keep all your money in one place—and access it almost anytime—without worrying that it may all go up in flames if your cat knocked over a candle.

$ Help you Win at Adulting: having bank accounts lets you use money apps like Venmo, get your paychecks faster, open credit cards, and apply for loans in the future.

No bank is a perfect, solve-all-ya-problems system. But you can choose a bank account the way you choose your next phone, your next hairstyle, your next brunch spot. The way you bank can be deeply, hilariously personal. The way you bank can actually feel good.

But as with any choice, you've gotta know what you're working with first.

YOUR TWO BANK ACCOUNT BESTIES

Most banks offer two basic types of accounts: the checking account and the savings account. Both are pretty necessary to your money life, and both serve different purposes. At the risk of saying something hella cheesy like BaNk aCcOuNts aRe YoUr FRiEnDs—they kind of are. In, like, a really specific way.

Think about how different friends serve different functions in your life. Like, you don't go to your resident grumpy friend to hype you up, right? And you don't go to your hype-man friend if you need to be petty and gossip a li'l. But you do need both, because ~balance.~

Applying the same super-scientific method here: picture your checking account as the hyper friend and your savings account as the (lovable) grump.

The Checking Account—AKA the Theater Kid

The checking account is the account that gets all the action. This is where you typically park the money you use for everyday, living-your-life spending.

When you open a checking account, you usually get something called a debit card—a plastic card with a bar on the back that looks annoyingly a lot like a credit card but acts very differently.

You use your debit card to spend whatever's in your checking account, and most stores, restaurants, and online shops accept debit cards from any bank.

You can put money into a checking account—or **deposit** money—by:

- $ Bringing cash to your bank or to certain ATMs
- $ Bringing an actual paper check to your bank or to certain ATMs
- $ Getting it transferred digitally from another bank account or via direct deposit, like when your employer sends your paycheck directly to your account.

You can take money out of a checking account—or **withdraw** money—by:

$ Getting cash from your bank or from ATMs

$ Writing those actual-paper checks to other people

$ Spending it on your debit card, either online, via an app, or in person

Now, think of your checking account as a theater kid—like, the lovable kind whose energy you can vibe with. They're exciting and dramatic, in a good but sometimes intense way. Just like this friend seems to have endless energy for a ton of social stuff, a checking account is built for those erry-dang-day Needs and Wants.

THE CHECKING THEATER KID

But you know how with dramatic friends, a bad mood can turn into an emotional spiral? The checking account does the exact same thing when you try to spend more money than you have. This meltdown is called The Overdraft (shudder), which, you'll remember, is what led to my Shame Cracker meltdown.

An overdraft fee goes like this: if you spend more money than what's actually in your account, like you have $10, but you try to buy something that costs $15? Boom. They charge you a certain fee—typically between $10 and $35—on top of that purchase, even if you don't have any money left.

And some banks will keep charging you that fee, and keep digging your negative hole deeper, until you deposit enough money to get your account back above $0. They might even close your account and summon legal powers to get you to pay them back. No bueno.

Some banks will offer to waive the fee if you connect your checking and savings account, so that instead of overdrafting, it'll pull money automatically from your savings to cover the hole. (A dangerous game, not just because it disturbs your savings' slumber, but also because sometimes they'll charge you a fee for *that*, too.)

I pretend they named it "checking" because you *should* be checking this account almost daily to avoid all that overdraft drama. Most banks have a mobile app, so I started making it a rule to check my bank apps before I open another app I use every day, like my favorite social media platform. Feels good to keep an eye on this hyper dude.

The Savings Account—AKA the Lovable Emo

All right, volume down, y'all—the savings account loves you, but as your lovable emo friend, they need you and your checking account to /sssshhhhhh./

Your lovable emo friend doesn't like a lot of action. It's all low lights and indoor voices. Don't ask them to go on adventures with you; they like their bed too much. But they are super loyal, and they're a friend for life.

That's the idea behind a savings account: This is where you park your Dream money, or any money that you don't plan on moving

THE SAVINGS EMO

for a long time. Savings accounts have a few lovably emo characteristics that work better for your Dream-type goals.

With a savings account, you can deposit as many times as you want. But be careful when you withdraw; many banks limit you to four to six withdrawals per month. Any more than that and you'll get hit with—sing it with me—a fee. (It's like: you can only text Emo Friend four to six times per month. Bother them too much and Emo will sue you for emotional damages.)

You won't get a debit card for a savings account, much like Emo Friend won't tell you his address so you can never try to visit. If you want to access money in your savings account, you've got to deposit or withdraw money through the bank, either in person or online.

THIS IS WHERE THINGS GET . . . INTEREST-ING

Besides withdrawals, the only other major difference between a checking and savings account is a liiiiiittle thing called interest. (I apologize on behalf of the universe for yet another very confusing name.)

To help explain this, I hit up my smart money friend Paco de Leon, founder of Hell Yeah bookkeeping, to explain.

PACO DE LEON

- ˅ SHE/HER
- ˅ QUEER
- ˅ DAUGHTER OF FILIPINO IMMIGRANTS, FIRST IN FAMILY TO GRADUATE COLLEGE

> PACO. PLS. Why are banks always yelling about "interest"?

> What dis? Are they trying to date me??

I got you. When it comes to money, interest actually has two definitions ✌️, but for now, we'll focus on interest for savings accounts 💸 specifically.

> I'm already sweating?

Nah—in the savings world, interest is a good thing. When you put your money in a savings account, the bank PAYS YOU bits of money—aka 💰 interest 💰.

When we're talking about saving accounts, interest is basically free money. 💰

The bank pays me?! CUTE.

. . . Wait, now I'm suspicious. Why are they paying me?

Is it like a thank-you gift? Do I have to pay it back?!

Nope. Banks pay you interest to encourage you to keep your money there. A bank will offer you interest as a pretty small percentage, or "annual rate"—for example, 0.07%.

That basically means they'll take whatever money is in your savings, 🗒 multiply it by 0.07%, and that's how much they'll add to your account.

. . . Am I supposed to get excited about such a tiny percentage, or—

I knoooow. The average US savings interest rate in Oct. 2022 was—wait for it—0.21%.

But let's say you put $5,000 into a savings account and it has 0.21% interest, right?

$5,000 x 0.21% = $10.50. Since interest rates are usualy applied annually, or once per year, you can earn $10.50 interest in the first year.

Typically, the bank will spread that $10.50 over a year, so you might get $0.87 in interest per month, for 12 months.

It's not a lot, but, hey—it's free money for doing nothing.

True. Free money is my favorite money.

So I'll just get $10.50 for free, every year, forever, if I leave my money in my savings account?

Yes!

Many banks offer a specific type of savings called a **High Yield Savings Account** (HYSA), which is a fancy name for savings accounts that got that good-good, super-high interest rate. HYSAs can have interest rates all the way up to 2% or more.

The catch with an HYSA? They usually have a minimum balance requirement—you can open a regular savings account with just $1, but for an HYSA you might have to keep $100 or $1,000 in there at all times, or else you get charged (sing it again!) a fee.

So, if you have a chunk of money that will be sitting there for a while—like a college savings or an emergency savings—it's smart to stick it in an HYSA so that your money can make the most money while you sleep. Teeny, tiny amounts, usually, but hey: free money is the best money[8].

So, let's run all that back real quick:

	CHECKING	SAVINGS
Can I withdraw every day?	Yup!	Nope; typically 4–6 per month
Can I deposit every day?	Yup!	Yup!
Do I get a debit card to carry around and spend?	Yup!	Nope.
What's the interest rate?	Usually none, occasionally super-low; on average, 0.06%	Li'l higher, from 0.15%–2%

WHICH BANK SHOULD I PICK?

Whew, baby (cracks knuckles); now we're really getting into the options. Different banks offer different things to help you organize your money better, depending on what's important to you. You can

---

8 LISTEN, I KNOW HOW RIDICULOUS THIS ALL SOUNDS. But adult-hood is hard. This is how we get our kicks now.

also choose a bank for the impact it has on your community and the world. Sweet, right? With all these options, choosing a bank is a lot like choosing a college.

Banks and colleges actually have a lot in common: They are often big concrete buildings filled with old stuff (cash, people, etc.) and they really, really want to take your money. So we should get to know our options better. Allow me to take you on a tour.

THREE STOPS ON BERNA'S
BANK TOUR

FIRST STOP: Big Bank University

$ **Population:** Seemingly everyone and their literal mama

$ **Location:** Typically squished between every Trendy Coffee Shop and Asian Fusion Thing

Like big-name colleges—Stanford! University of Texas! Michigan State!—you might've heard about these banks before. These are your Chases, your Wells Fargos, your Bank of Americas—the banks you see driving through basically any town, anywhere.

You might be a Big Bank University person if:

$ **You love a good brick building.** Big banks often have branches—aka physical locations—in nearly every town, which is great if you prefer in-person interaction or expect to be handling cash and checks pretty often.

$ **You like customer service convenience.** Big banks = big budgets = they can afford to give you that 24/7 top-notch customer service. This is clutch if you plan on traveling a ton and want to be able to talk to a human when you drop your debit card in a gutter in Thailand at midnight. For example.

$ **You like bells 'n' whistles.** Y'know how big universities are more likely to have all kinds of student orgs or attract celebs to campus events? Big banks are more likely to have the most updated tech to help you with your money, like easier-to-use apps, better online tools, or more types of accounts.

You probably would not love Big Bank University if:

$ **You hate fees.** How do you think big banks pay for all them branches, good tech, and 24/7 customer service? YOUR MONEY. To pay for all of this, they're more likely to charge you mad fees and sometimes pay you less in interest. (More on this in a bit.)

$ **You don't like crowds.** Big banks have millions of customers, and they often don't have time to treat you like the precious sunflower you are. They're less likely to make exceptions, bend rules, or give that local-community-cozy touch.

$ **You want to sidestep the problematic.** Big banks are much more likely to appear on the news under headlines like "Turns out Big Bank was secretly funding this Terrible Thing that Destroys the Planet!" Googling "Any Big Bank's name + scandal" can be pretty horrifying.

SECOND STOP: Online Bank Polytechnic School

$ **Population:** Whoever is closest to the Wi-Fi router
$ **Location:** Wherever the signal is the strongest

Make room for the new kids in town—but, like, hella room, because there's a new kid every ten seconds. Online banks exist entirely on the internet, kinda like those online-only technical schools where you can get your degree from your couch. There are no buildings; your money is held 100% digitally.

You might enroll in Online Bank Polytechnic if:

$ **You're super techy.** You appreciate a sleek app or website with a ton of features. Online banks are more likely to move fast with updates, giving you every fintech bell and whistle. Plus, you can access your money basically anywhere you know the Wi-Fi password.

$ **You hate fees.** Online bank = no buildings. With less physical stuff to pay for, they don't typically charge you as many fees. Just like how online colleges are often cheaper than big universities, online banks are more likely to offer super-low-fee or no-fee accounts.

$ **You've got a strong social conscience.** Online banks—which often have younger and more diverse founders and staff—are more likely to be outspoken about political and social issues. You might see an online bank hop on social media and address racism, for example, whereas big banks tend to keep quiet.

You might wanna skip Online Bank Polytechnic if:

- $ **You really need that in-person vibe.** If you use cash often for work—like if you get tips from a restaurant—depositing can get tricky. With online banks, there's no physical location and nowhere for you to stick the cash. You may have to find a special deposit-accepting ATM, grab a money order—basically an old-school way to turn cash into digital money, but with a fee—or give it to a friend who can send you the digital funds.

- $ **You want all the options, right now.** Once upon a time, I really wanted to use this awesome new online bank—let's call it MoneyLand—because I loved their mission and their vibe. But I like opening a ton of different accounts to stay organized. Since MoneyLand was so new, they didn't have the manpower to let me open my fourteen+ accounts. Yet. Womp.

THIRD STOP: Credit Union Community College

- $ **Population:** The type of people who follow their senator on Twitter and show up to town hall meetings
- $ **Location:** In your city, next to Ye Olde Doughnut place, like, how is that place still open?

(I'm just gonna ask you to Google "Credit Union Mascots" real quick. Because THAT'S A THING.)

Pump the tour bus brakes—technically, a credit union is not a bank. Teeeeeechnically, credit unions are (Bad BBC Miniseries Extra voice) a not-for-profit money-making cooperative whose members can borrow from each other at low rates.

In English now! When you put your money in a big bank or an online bank, you're a customer. When you put your money in a credit union, you become a member—in other words, the whole idea is that you are treated a bit more like a part owner of the whole shebang.

Not everyone can roll up to any local credit union and hop on; credit unions are often formed for folks who have a specific connection with each other. There are credit unions for certain towns or cities, certain religions or cultural groups, even credit unions for certain careers, like military folks or health care workers. Credit unions are like your local community colleges. Big ol' emphasis on the community.

You might be down for a credit union if:

$ **You're about that community-care life.** Maybe you'd rather keep your money local and see it benefit the folks around you. When you deposit your money into a credit union, everyone's money is put in one big pool so that other members can get loans or other services. (But no, your bank account never gets smaller; your money is safe!)

- $ **No, foreal: you reaaaally don't get down with fees.** Banks are for-profit businesses, so they have to make a profit somehow. But since credit unions are not-for-profits, they don't have to pay certain taxes to the government, AND they are not required to make a profit; they exist to serve you. That means you're more likely to enjoy no or low fees, and awesome perks on credit cards and loans.

- $ **You want that hands-on feel.** You're a member, not a customer—and that means you've got special access that you don't get at a big or online bank. You might be able to do things like vote on the credit union's board of directors or decide what type of events they throw. A credit union is also more likely to offer community-specific support—like how some Latine-focused credit unions offer Spanish language budgeting classes.

A credit union might not be your jam if:

- $ **You are super-super-tech oriented.** Now, this isn't true for all credit unions—a ton of bigger credit unions have excellent apps and super-accessible customer  service. But historically, since credit unions are usually smaller, more niche, and not-for-profits, they may not have the most updated tech.

- $ **You need that 24/7 assistance.** In a community college, you can get help . . . as long as the office secretary, Ms. Brenda, is there between the hours of 10:00 a.m. and 1:00 p.m., every seventh Thursday. Samesies with many credit unions: they're more likely to be limited to business hours if you need help, but some larger credit unions do offer that 24/7 access.

$ **You want all the banking options.** It's like this: at the end of 2020, big ol' Bank of America had twenty-two different credit cards for you to choose from (hoo!)—while the Navy Federal Credit Union only offered six types. If you want to explore every type of account out there, some credit unions can't help you.

Do You Have to Stick to One Type of Bank?

Nope. I've used all types, sometimes at the same time. I'll change banks if I see lower fees or better features elsewhere or if a bank does shady stuff I don't agree with. For some reason, my parents thought having tons of accounts was low-key illegal and made me believe so, too—like when you turn the light on inside the car while driving—but it's not, and it's worth being able to choose the features that work for me.

Can You Leave a Bank If You're Not into It?

Yup. Do we leave relationships we're not into? I HOPE SO. Considering the way fintech keeps doling out more banks specific to our lifestyles, we can totally enjoy hopping around. Just make sure you don't owe your bank any remaining overdraft funds so that they don't hit you with any fees on your way out of the door.

$ TALK MONEY TO ME $
THREE THINGS YOU GOTTA ASK ANY BANK

Are You Insured?

This is a hard stop: you want to make sure any bank you mess with has insurance. Regular banks will have FDIC insurance. That's a fancy acronym for Federal Deposit Insurance Corporation—aka a part of the government that makes sure your money is protected.

The credit union version of this comes from the National Credit Union Share Insurance Fund, or the NCUSIF.

Insurance basically means: if this bank catches on fire; if this bank explodes in a mysterious radioactivity accident; if Rihanna tells the world this bank is trash and the social media backlash is so bad that the bank has to shrivel up and die . . . your money is safe, and you'll get your money back, typically up to a limit of $250,000.

What Are Your Fees?

In 2020, banks made $12.4 billion off regular customers like you and me, just from checking overdraft fees alone. And not all fees are created equal.

Every bank is different, but some (truly BS) fees to look for:

$ **Maintenance, Service or Management Fee:** A monthly fee for . . . literally just having the account. (I know.) Every month for basically no reason. Boom. Fee.

$ **Minimum Balance Fee:** If a bank says you have to keep a certain amount in your account at all times, like $100, and your balance ever dips below that? Boom. Fee.

$ **Overdraft or Non-Sufficient Funds Fee:** Like we mentioned earlier, if you spend more money than what's actually in your account? Boom. Fee. (The bank can keep charging you fees, close your account, and haunt you via collection agencies until you pay them back.)

$ **ATM Fee:** If you use an ATM that isn't specifically owned by your bank—like those random, crusty-dusty ATMs at the bodega. Boom. Fee. (But some banks reimburse that fee.)

. . . Whatcha Got for Me?

Last little treat: banks are always running limited-time promotions to incentivize people to open up accounts. I'm talking cash money, deposited directly into your new account, just to say thanks for joining up. You could get anywhere from $50 to $500, depending on the promotion. FREE. MONIES.

Some finance-hacking online resources update their site to show which banks have the best promotions going on that month. (Give something like "checking account promotion [insert month and year]" a spin on the Googles.) But it's always worth asking any bank you're sniffing at if they've got promos to offer, too.

HOW DO I OPEN MY OWN BANK ACCOUNT?

Here's the thing: you can't just roll through a bank and pick up an account, like a churro. (Insert dream sequence about how I wish banks gave out churros.) Most banks allow you to apply for an account online, and some require you to go their physical location and talk to a human, but with nearly every bank, there's a big, phat catch.

Banks ask for a lot of incredibly personal information. Like, without even going to dinner first.

At the bare minimum, most banks will ask you for:

$ Government proof of your name and date of birth to see if you're over the age of eighteen (like an ID or driver's license)

$ Proof of street address (like a bill, a lease, or government-issued ID)

$ An ID number (could be a Social Security Number [SSN], a driver's license number, or a ton of others)

Let us pause a moment here and unpack the plentiful ways this system is wack. With these requirements, many banks shut out the following people:

$ Teens without housing, or who are not close with their parents, or trying to escape abusive family relationships, or simply want to establish financial independence.

$ Any human under the age of eighteen who has to live with the knowledge that, in the UK, for example, you can open your own bank account as early as eleven years old. What?!

$ The estimated 10.5 million undocumented immigrants currently living, working, and paying taxes in the US who either don't have help getting alternative forms of ID or don't want to give up their personal information for (very justified) fear of deportation.

deep breath like my meditation apps taught me

Like I said, our banking system is definitely not perfect. The concept of banks is old—like, Italy-in-the-1400s old—and these rules can't always be changed very easily.

Later in the book, we'll dig into some ways to be part of the change, but for now, we've gotta navigate these weird waters together.

What If I'm Over Eighteen?

If you've got a Social Security Number, then you have the privilege of choosing basically any bank in the United States. Mentally thank the universe, and take a sec to consider the millions of folks around you who will have a harder time banking without it.

What If I'm Under Eighteen?

You'll need some type of parent, guardian, or adult to open one with you. And that adult will need to show some government-issued ID, too.

If you can round up a supportive adult, you can sniff into the options below, and remember: financial experts are always creating new lists of resources online, so hit the Googles to see the latest.

$ **Custodial Accounts:** This is a bank account that an adult opens for you, but it's as stuffy as it sounds—you don't get a ton of control. Typically, only your Adult can deposit or withdraw money, and they can only use the money on You-related things. Once you are old enough according the account's terms and your state's laws, whatever money is in there is officially released to you.

$ **Joint Accounts:** You and the Adult co-own this account, and you get much more control—it's like a bank account on training wheels. You get your own debit card, and both you and the Adult can deposit and withdraw freely. Some banks even offer awesome apps where the Adult can help you set up a budget or track goals. The Adult has the power to look at your spending at any time; they may also be able to connect their bank account to send you money or help fix any issues.

$ **Prepaid debit cards:** This isn't technically an account—this is more like a bank-y gift card. An Adult loads up their own money onto a debit card, and you get to spend it. Like a gift card, you typically can't spend more than what your Adult put on the card—the purchase might just get declined, or, as usual: feeeeees.

$ **Student Accounts:** Loophole alert! If you can prove that you're actively enrolled in college, some banks offer Student Accounts that you can open without an adult. Student  accounts usually come decked out with awesome features meant for folks who are banking for the first time—it might have low or no monthly fees, no fees to use an ATM, or special tools to help you save money.

How Do I Talk to My Family about Getting a Bank Account?

Maybe you need your family's help to open a bank account—but what if your family doesn't usually discuss money? As we'll unpack throughout the book, different cultures and generations have different feels about money, and it's worth being mindful about your approach—even as an adult, I know I'd get slapped with the chinela if I came on too strong. But having that first money convo with your family doesn't have to be scary.

Before you approach your fam, have a lil' think: What's important to your family, and how will your new bank account help with that?

$ If they're big on safety and security, tell them how your money won't get stolen in an account. If they're worried you'll spend wildly, dazzle them with your new knowledge of joint accounts or prepaid debit cards, where they can have some control while still giving you bank experience.

$ If your family is like mine—big on achievement and succeeding in American culture—tell them exactly how it would help you succeed. I told my family I needed two bank accounts for school (which I did), that it would help me be smarter with money sooner, and I wouldn't have to ask them for money help later. Boom.

$ If you think they'll shoot you down, come prepared. Brainstorm the pros and cons, and try something like: "I get that you may be worried because . . . but here's how I planned for that." This shows that you were responsible enough to consider the downsides, too.

What If I or My Family Is Undocumented?

Navigating the finance world while undocumented can feel real friggin' intimidating. It's hard to know which banks will protect your privacy—and it's even harder to find resources to guide us. That's why I brought in my smarter friends: Adina Appelbaum, Esq., and Mauricio Castillo Ferri of Immigrant Finance.

TEXTSPERT

ADiNA APPELBAUM, ESQ.:

- SHE/HER
- iMMiGRATiON ATTORNEY
- GREAT-GRANDDAUGHTER OF REFUGEES

MAURiCiO CASTiLLO FERRi:

- HE/HiM
- PROUD iMMiGRANT FROM ECUADOR

> Adina! Mauricio! Even in my deepest Google searches, I'm strugggggling to find solid info about Banking While Undocumented. ☕

> What do undocumented folks need to know if they're unsure about opening up bank accounts?

Adina

> Here's the truth: there are no legal requirements saying someone must be a US citizen to have a bank account.

Folks who are undocumented CAN have access to some of the best bank accounts out there.

But nearly every bank is like WhAt'S uR SoCiaL SeCuRiTy—

Mauricio

The key is having an 💳 Individual Tax Identification Number (ITIN) 💳—it's like an alternative to the Social Security Number.

You can apply for free through the Internal Revenue Service, or the IRS.

. . . I mean, what about privacy? Is that safe??

Adina

It can definitely be scary to think about sending your info to a government agency like the IRS, but keep in mind: the 🏛 IRS 🏛 is a separate agency from any immigration agencies.

There are strong privacy laws in place that stop the IRS from sharing info with other agencies; a whole new law would need to be passed to change that.

WHEW. 'Kay. So we'd be good with an ITIN?

Mauricio

Yup—millions of undocumented folks use their ITINs to open accounts and pay taxes every year.

Most national banks accept an ITIN, but if you're not sure, practice becoming an advocate and ask first.

Wha' bout budgeting apps, and stuff that asks for your bank information?

Can we trust 'em?

Adina

While there is always risk to sharing sensitive info with third parties like apps, these types of software typically have strong security features to protect privacy.

We think the benefits outweigh the risk, because these tools can really take your finances to the next level. 📊

Mauricio

It never hurts to ask about any company's privacy features. Banking might take a bit more effort, but all undocumented families deserve to be on a path to build financial stability and wealth.

TRUE. THAT. 👏 ▶ 🔊

A few other resources for undocumented folks, to start you down your rabbit hole:

$ **Specialized accounts:** Credit unions like DC Credit Union offer their SAFE Accounts for folks who don't have an SSN or an ITIN; they accept government IDs from other countries, and they offer other dope resources like non-English language assistance and low-cost wire transfers if you need to send money abroad.

$ **Specialized programs:** Any of the 108 nationwide credit unions that belongs to Juntos Avanzamos, a program that focuses on banking for Latine communities, accept alternate forms of identification and documentation—and they offer financial education resources in Spanish.

$ **Non-bank banking:** Services like Transact at participating 7-Elevens allow you to sign up for a prepaid debit card and receive direct deposits—so you can get paid and use debit card–required services, like Venmo, without needing a bank account.

SO DO I JUST GET, LIKE, ONE OF EACH ACCOUNT?

Remember your Needs, Wants, and Dreams dollars from chapter 2? Once you've chosen a bank, take a look at your budgeting plan. Then, open as many accounts as you need to organize your budgeting categories. People always *dramatic gasp* when I show first-time budgeters screenshots of my bank accounts—I have at least seven accounts open at all times, a mix of checking and savings, and I'm always changing up my categories. For some reason, many of us were taught that having several bank accounts is a bad thing, but at this level of organization, it has saved my budgeting butt.

I recommend starting with one account for each of your budget jobs:

1. One checking account for your Needs
2. One checking account for your Wants
3. One savings account for your Dreams

During your CFO meetings/budgeting sessions, you can open up your three bank accounts and transfer your paycheck money, your random gift money, every other dollar you've got, to your different accounts—and keep distributing until every dollar has a job.

Once you're comfortable with that, you can open more accounts for any section of your money life. I'm a big fan of the Parking Lot account: one checking account where any dollar you get stops first, before driving off to its specific Needs, Wants, Dreams account. Having this makes it way easier to track and distribute your monies till every dollar is gone.

And now, probably my actual favorite part of banking, in general:

You Must Nickname Your Account. (Foreal.)

This may seem trivial, but I cannot stress enough how much this tiny trick helped me: you are probably able to nickname your different bank accounts online. And you can name 'em whatever you want. *maniacal villain muahaha*

Not only will it keep your money organized and make your finances feel so much more personal, but it's such a mental money game changer. Because, listen: Do you know how excited I get to deposit money in my "When I Move U Move-ing Fund"? Do you know how entertaining it is to hear my bank's customer service go, "Ms. Anat, will we be making that deposit to your . . . uh . . . 'Beach Better Have My Money' Savings?"

It's envisioning your goal. It's the feeling of control. It's banking with a sprinkle of (potentially inappropriate) humor, which is the only way I ever wanna bank.

OPEN MIC

I don't know if you could tell, but I . . . am basically a child in an Adult Skin Suit. That's why I get so hype when people tell me their super-personal or ridiculous bank account nicknames—it makes me feel like we're all little kids grabbing free lollipops in some big, serious bank (OF LIFE 😂). Like we're not supposed to be having this much financial fun. Which is my favorite kind of fun.

So lemme pass the mic to some folks in my online community—maybe their brilliant bank account nickname ideas will spark some of your own.

I asked my Money Friends: What kinds of nicknames have you given your bank accounts?

🎤 "'Teetus Deletus' (for my top surgery saving) and 'Ratattooie' (for tattoos, of course)." —Marve A.

🎤 "All my accounts are named after songs from my Pinay idol, Ruby Ibarra: 'pLAYBILL$,' 'SKIES,' 'ROLL CALL.'" —Evelyn O.

🎤 "If you touch, you better be dying." —Megan F.

🎤 "My credit card is called 'Nah.'" —Nicole

🎤 "'Shake Your ___ on a Yacht.' (If you don't recognize the meme, I highly recommend Googling.)" —Greisy H.

🎤 "'Make It Rain' (for incoming $) and 'When the ___ Hits the Fan' (for unexpected large things)." —Christie C.

Does My Bank Make Me a Bad Person?

Hard truth: as much as we love to bank, sometimes our banks behave badly. If you see news about your bank being sketchy and are wondering, "Am I a crappy person if I choose this bank? Is Berna gonna judge me for throwing my money at the bank closest to my job?" The answer: absolutely not.

Remember when we talked about capitalism in chapter 1, and how it means that nearly everything revolves around money, for better or for worse? The truth is, someone is being exploited with nearly every money decision you make. Another truth: you gotta do what you gotta do to survive in the world as it is. Both are complicated, and both are true.

It's not a perfect system, so your options won't be perfect, either. But when we understand our options, we can make more empowered choices for our lives; we gain more power than we had before.

And we need all the power and choices we can get, because if we look back through history?

We've been getting systematically stripped of that power for centuries.

PIT STOP: THE UNBANKING OF BLACK AND BROWN PEOPLE

When I first started learning about all these banking options, I got super excited about this new financial life. But I also got really curious: Why didn't my parents know this stuff? Why didn't they teach me?

I told my family about how I started opening up more bank accounts, and they were . . . kinda horrified. "Doesn't that lower your credit score?" (No.) "Don't you have to pay for all those accounts?" (No!) "What if they take all your money? Why don't you just keep your savings at home?!" (DAD.)

I was like, WHA. Where is all of this distrust and misinformation coming from? I did some searching, and y'all—what I found changed my entire perspective on money.

GET IN CUTIES, WE'RE LEARNING ABOUT THE SYSTEMIC FINANCIAL DISEMPOWERMENT OF BLACK AND BROWN PEOPLE!

I learned that in 2019, the Federal Reserve said that 6% of adults in the US are unbanked—aka they don't have a bank account. But according to the Bangko Sentral ng Pilipinas—a major bank in the Philippines—71% of adults in the Philippines are unbanked.

I was like, WHA?!

The more I started talking about money to other folks in my Filipinx community, the more I heard stories about:

$ How the US and Japanese governments sent colonizing forces to capture Philippine cities during World War II, stealing and destroying nearly $20.5 million in Filipino wealth during the 1945 Battle of Manila.

$ How these invaders specifically targeted banks in the financial hubs of the Philippines—and, since many of these banks were uninsured, generations of life earnings and savings disappeared.

$ How so many of our grandparents kept their money hidden at home—under mattresses, in urns, in emptied-out Bibles—because they lost their wealth in that disaster and stopped trusting banks.

Then I was like, OH.

This mistrust—and, because of that, miseducation—has been passed down from generation to generation. All the way down through my family, all the way to me.

I learned about how even though only 6% of adults in the US don't have a bank account, when you break it down by race and ethnicity, only 3% of white adults are unbanked—while 10% of Hispanic adults and 14% of Black adults are unbanked.

Everyone now: I was like, WHA?!

But then I cracked open books like *The Color of Money* by Mehrsa Baradaran, and read about:

$ How the Freedman's Bank of 1865—created so that formerly enslaved Black folks, primarily sharecroppers, could keep their wages safe—closed less than a decade later due to corruption. Why? Freedman's white leaders were only giving loans to white people. Over 38% of Black Freedman's customers lost their money. In today's dollars, that's nearly $22 million of many Black families' first-ever wealth, gone forever.

$ How there used to be a hub of thriving Black banks—Black Wall Street, they called it—in Tulsa, Oklahoma, in the 1920s. Then a mob of white racists tore through the neighborhood, killing hundreds of Black residents and destroying over one thousand buildings and millions of dollars in Black wealth.

$ How racist US policies persisted—like how Black World War II veterans were denied the same GI Bill benefits that helped white veterans pay for school, buy homes, and build wealth.

DAAAAAAANG! Then I was like, OHHH.

Considering all of this, maybe that's why the most marginalized folks choose not to trust banks. We see a disturbing echo in the way racist capitalist powers have destroyed worldwide BIPOC wealth throughout time. This effed up US financial history repeats itself for Latine folks, Indigenous and Native American folks, Asian and Pacific Islander folks . . . see where I'm going here?

Here's the thing: we have way more options and access to education than our parents and grandparents had. There are more BIPOC folks in fintech, which means more banks and services created with our needs—and lived experiences—in mind.

While we're on the hunt for better banks, here are a few other things we can keep in mind:

$ **Who are the human faces behind these banks?** How diverse is their C-Suite—the CEO, the CFO, the C-whatevers—and are they indeed all old white dudes?

$ **Are they impact-minded?** Climate change disproportionately affects marginalized groups. Is your bank aware of its environmental footprint? Does it have certified B Corporation status, which means it scored high in transparency and awareness of their impact on their employees and the earth?

$ **Do they walk their talk?** Have they ever donated to a cause you care about? If they ever claimed to launch any Diversity,

Equity, and Inclusion (DEI) initiatives, did they actually follow through? Run their name through a Google News search—have they been dragged in the news for some other action that makes your stomach turn?

I've come a long way since my Shame Cracker days, but sometimes I still think about that sad intern Berna, wiping her tears on her Forever 21 pencil skirt. I wish I could travel back in time, take her hand, and lead her to the nearest free Wi-Fi to search better banking options. But I know she was doing her best with what she knew.

And, when my mom steered sixteen-year-old me to her own Big Bank's counter to open my first checking account, she was doing her best, too. She was passing down the limited options she knew. That's all any of us can do.

But that's the magic of intergenerational wealth: we're not just trying to pass down dollars. We're trying to pass down knowledge. Knowledge is wealth because knowledge means options. And when we gain access to more options, we can make more intentional choices to start busting these biased systems on our own terms. We can choose our money systems with our head, our gut, and our whole entire chest.

So while it can feel overwhelming to decide where to put your money among the zillions of options, there's one question that will never steer you wrong: Who—and what—is worth it to you? That's your choice, and yours alone.

WAIT, WHAT?

We love bank-ific organization, but trying to choose from all the banking options in the world can feel like putting your brain in a financial blender. Here's a lil' cheat sheet for what we've learned in this chapter.

How to find the right bank for you:

$ Get familiar with the difference between checking and savings accounts, and how interest can help you get free money (starting on page 71).

$ Make a list of what's important to you in a bank–and then see if a big bank, online bank, credit union or some combo fits your list (starting on page 80).

$ Map out the things you need to open a bank account: Are you over eighteen? Do you have a government identification number? Check out your options starting on page 90.

$ Start off with three bank accounts for your Needs, Wants, and Dreams. Give 'em nicknames, and next time you get money, practice transferring all your dollars into those new accounts.

$ Get curious about the history of banking in your family or culture. Is there any distrust or misinformation about banks in your community? Who can help you dig into the "why"? (Head back to chapter 1, page 20, for tips on getting elders to talk!)

4

HELLA FREEDOM
(AKA SAVING MONEY)

The best thing I ever, ever saved money for . . . was the chance to sleep in a bed with five dogs in South Korea. Allow me to (literally) set the scene.

HECTIC REWIND SOUNDS AND SQUIGGLY VISUALS!

SCENE: The year is 2016. Berna and her future boo are sitting at a two-top at Little Star Pizza in San Francisco. It's Date #3. Berna's new personal finance hype is deep. So are her visible sweat stains.

BERNA: So, uh . . . do you have . . . like . . . debt? (very fast, not breathing) Cause I'm like $50,000 in debt. HaHAhaHAaaaa crazy-rightanyway how bouchu?!

BOO: . . . Yeah.

BERNA: Do you . . . want to pay that debt off eventually?

BOO: . . . Yeah.

BERNA: (deep breath) Okay, wild idea, totally say no if you want—what if we, like, learn money stuff and pay them off together, and then, save up a ton to do something big? Like . . . quit our jobs? And travel the world? For no reason?

BOO: . . . (chewing) . . . Yeah.

HECTIC FORWARD SOUNDS AND SQUIGGLY VISUALS!

SMASH CUT OF A BUNCH OF SUPER SHORT SCENES!

$ Berna ugly-crying and submitting her last student loan payment, ever.

$ Boo seeing our travel savings account hit $36,000 and yelling "BABE, WE DID IT!"

$ Both, in pajamas, clicking Submit Payment for one-way tickets to New Zealand.

$ Both snoring in a bed while dogsitting five pups in South Korea, a pup nestled in each of their crevices.

AAAAAND SCENE.

If this were a travel commercial with a cheesy tagline, it would be: Saving money unlocks your wildest effing dreams. And the truth is, whether your dream is to buy stuff, buy experiences, or buy time, everyone is saving money for one thing: freedom.

LIVIN' THE DREAM

Because, look: when former Boo and I were saving money to pay off our debt and travel the world, our top priority was not finding the best blackwater rafting spot in New Zealand, or the fanciest hot spring spa in Kyoto. (Though thanks to our savings, I now have recs for both. ✌️)

We saved money so we could have the friggin' priceless experience of buying a one-way ticket with no real plans. So we could, at least once in our young-ish lives, ditch the work-world hamster wheel and make it up as we go. We wanted to afford to live out our greatest fantasy: doing whatever we wanted. The five-dogs-in-South-Korea-type adventures were a cute bonus.

In this capitalistic simulation we call Life, saving money = earning the freedom to Buy That Thing Guilt-Free, to Leave That Town, to Earn That Degree, or even to simply sleep peacefully at night knowing you've got a financial cushion if, say, two over-excited American travelers break your toaster. (I have recs for replacement toasters, too.)

We save money to get free, and that's what I want your savings to do for you. I know we could all use more freedom in our lives. I've got three main steps to help us start saving money—and we're gonna have a good time doing it, too.

But before we go anywhere, we gotta zoom in on one important truth.

MAYBE YOU JUST NEED TO GET PAID MORE

There's one giant thing stopping most of us from saving money. It's not your emotions, it's not your education, and it's not even those offensively accurate targeted ads on IG.

Sometimes you don't need savings tips or tricks. Sometimes you just need more money.

Saving money, at the core, is about math. Just like we saw in our Budgeting chapter, the math has to math. You have to earn more than what your life costs in order to save money. If all your dollars are too busy keeping you alive, then you literally have nothing to save for later.

Don't get me wrong: all the tips we're about to go through helped me save money in massive ways. But the #1 thing that helped me and my former boo hit our $36,000 Quit Life to Travel goal in just two years?

A bigger paycheck. Dassit. I got a new job that paid me almost twice as much as my old job. Once I earned more, I had plenty of dollars to cover my survival, so I had plenty of leftover dollars to save. All the tips and tricks just made the process run faster and feel more fun.

This might seem obvious, but it's important to remember: too many of us are quick to internalize our money problems and beat ourselves up when we're just straight-up underpaid. You might be beating yourself up about being BaD aT sAviNg MoNeY for No. Freaking. Reason.

Look at your paycheck first. Nothing helps you get to your savings goal faster than earning more money. Earning a bigger paycheck is like taking a plane from San Francisco to New York, as opposed to tryna get there via broken Razor scooter.[9]

And that, friends, is why my three steps to saving money are in this specific order:

1. Earn more than what you need to survive each month.
2. Get hella specific with your savings goal.
3. And finally, this is mandatory: make that shiz so enjoyable for yourself that you'll legitimately want to save money. All. The. Time.

BE NICE TO MY FRIEND (YOU)

---

9 Also, any ~financial experts~ who try to tell you that your mindset is the main problem? They're probably trying to sell you their bootleg mastermind course for $YeahRight.99.

EARN MORE THAN WHAT YOU NEED TO SURVIVE

Saving requires a stream of income—i.e., you need to be receiving money on a regular degular basis. (I think the ancient Greeks called it a . . . job?) Remember back in the Budgeting chapter, where we calculated your Entire Life Bill, the amount you need to be earning each month for your bare minimums? Yeah. You gotta be earning more money than that.

Now, if you aren't earning enough to put aside some Dream funds, there are a lot of things you can do. But for now, here are some rabbit holes to go down:

$ **If you've got a job, ask for a raise,** and come prepared with solid evidence re: why they should pay you more. Can you pull up receipts on  how your work earned the company more money, more eyeballs, more success? Or how a staff change meant that you took on more work, and now you need to get paid equal to your new responsibilities?

$ **Consider the side hustle.** A side hustle is essentially creating a second job—if you have the time!—when the first one doesn't pay enough. Typically, that means turning an interest or hobby into a money-making project. More on this in a bit.

$ **Get credentials or a degree that will help you land a higher-paying job.** A study by Northeastern University showed that on average, when you earn a higher degree, your salary can jump up as much as $19,000 per year. But watch the math here. As we'll see in chapter 5, school debt can be hella expensive, so it's important to ask yourself: How much will that certificate or degree cost, and will you really get paid enough to cover that debt later?

$ **Punch up for higher minimum wage.** Look to your leaders. Bust a hole in your local politician's inbox to raise the friggin' minimum wage where you live. Get your vote on. Show up at those local town hall meetings and ask questions. Join a local organizing group already dedicated to financial inequity in your town. Fight to make real change not just for your paycheck, but everyone else's. (We dedicated all of chapter 7 to stuff like this.) And while you're doing that . . .

$ **Become an average white man.** Oops. But now that we're here—we do know that according to LeanIn.org, for every $1 a man earns in the US, a woman earns 79 cents, right? And when you take race into account: many Black, Latine, Asian, Pacific Islander, and Indigenous women women earn as little as 55 cents to the white man's dollar? HmhMM.

$ TALK MONEY TO ME $
KNOWING WHEN TO QUIT

When it comes to earning a paycheck, there is way too much hype behind "Blah blah loyalty, find your passion, stick to it and it'll pay off," etc. In reality, leaving a job could be the best thing for your earning power.

Next time some coffee-breather wags a finger at you about quitting, hit 'em with these facts:

$ According to MarketWatch, the average raise can get you a 3% bump in your pay—but changing jobs usually gets you a 10 to 20% bump. That's why one of the best ways to earn more money is to leave your job for a higher-paid one—ideally, when you've already got that higher-paid job lined up.

$ Your job does not have to be your passion. In fact, according to a 2019 study by Deloitte, 80% of Americans do not feel passionate about their jobs and are just trying to earn money to live. It's almost like the idea of tying your personal life passion to your means of survival in this unfair system was . . . a lie? Sometimes, the right job is simply the one paying you right now.

$ Quitting is a movement. According to financial educator and Yahoo! Money writer Mandi Woodruff-Santos, American workers find a new job roughly every two to three years, holding over a dozen jobs between the ages of eighteen and fifty-two. And that was before the "Great Resignation," when a record 4 million Americans quit their jobs in 2021 looking for better pay, better flexibility, better mental health. Translation? You're. Not. Alone.

Give it a think, discuss this with your group chat, or find me on the Internets and Talk Money To Me: If you had enough savings to quit your job or school, what would you do next?

STEP TWO
GET HELLA SPECIFIC

Hard financial pill to swallow: just saying "I want to save money" will not help you save money. RIGHT? THE INJUSTICE.

Pretend you're a rideshare driver and I got into your car. You're like, "Where to, your eminence?" And I'm like, "Idk, I just wanna . . . go." ?!!? Exactly. You need details, an address, a dropped pin, for frick's sake. You need that same type of hella-specific direction when saving money.

~~I want to save money~~

WHO/WHAT/WHERE/WHEN/WHY

I deposit $60 in my Beep Beep Bye Betches savings account every other Friday because I want to drive my own car outta this town by September 2030.

That's what I meant by hella specific. The most effective savings goal serves up exact financial coordinates. It has a WHO, WHAT, WHERE, WHEN, and WHY.

WHO: That's You. Boom, Easy Win.

(You felt that little serotonin bump just now? Remember that.)

WHAT: Exactly What Amount of Dollars Are You Saving Each Month?

Get yourself to the Googles and type in "**free savings calculator.**" A savings calculator will ask you a few important questions: How much money do you want to save? How much money do you have right now? When do you want to hit your goal?

Once you plug all those in—you can play around; the numbers don't have to be perfect—the savings calculator will tell you exactly how much you need to put away every month to reach that goal. It's basically giving you a pretend savings "bill" that you have to "pay" yourself every month to hit your goal. (I love when bots do the math for me.)

Let's say the savings calculator says your monthly savings "bill" is $100. The question you gotta ask your budget and yourself: Can I afford that $100 savings bill?

If your answer is no, then skip back to Step One and focus on your income. Can you earn more to cover that savings bill? Can you snip parts of your monthly budget, even temporarily, to reach it?

Once you know how you'll be paying your savings bill, we can move on to Where.

WHERE: Exactly WHERE Is Your Saved Money Gonna Live?

Keep a dedicated savings account specifically for your goal, totally separate from the rest of your money. As we said on page 79, High Yield Savings Accounts are clutch for goals like this. You might even keep your savings at a separate bank from your checking account, to avoid the temptation to withdraw.

Oh, and don't forget to nickname it, too. Personally, I've found that the more the name makes me laugh, or is something meaningful to me, the more likely I am to actually save. I've named my savings accounts:

$ Operation Yeehaw (That was my savings for a BFF vacay in Austin.)

$ Eff Off Fund (That was my "can't wait to quit my job" savings.)

$ NO BERNA NO TOUCHIES TILL NOV (That was my holiday savings.)

$ Love's Eternal Glory (*Office* fans in the house? Shared savings with my former boo.)

WHEN: When Are You Gonna Deposit / When Are You Done?

When #1: When, exactly, are you gonna beep-boop-beep hit Deposit and transfer money to your savings each month?

If you figured out your budget from chapter 2, you can add your savings bill to your list of monthly Needs. That way, you'll treat it like any other bill and deposit it to your savings as a part of your biweekly budgeting sesh/CFO meeting. Just like a utility bill, pretend someone's gonna come and track you down if you don't pay it. You could even kick your budgeting sesh off with a deposit, just to start things off on a happy lil' serotonin bump.

Remember when we said saving money is like paying yourself first? When I deposit to my savings, I love acting like I'm sticking money in the pocket of my Future Self, especially if it's for a trip. If the goal is Vacay in Miami, for example, I'm like: (Hits Deposit) That's a highly Grammable mocktail on me, girl. (Hits Deposit) That's to tip the hot pool boi. (Hits Deposit) Go ahead and get the additional guac, Future-beautiful, you're on vacation, and we have that Add Guac money nooooow.

And When #2: When will you hit your goal and celebrate your massive win? The savings calculator should be able to tell you the exact-ish date you'll hit your finish line. Stick that date in your calendar, plan a Moment for that day. No, seriously. Because if our society celebrates babies, weddings, and graduations, we should also be celebrating hitting a major money move. You earned that.

WHY: Exactly Why Are You Saving This Money?

This is the most important detail, y'all—it's the Thing that will keep you motivated when all the other Things just aren't inspiring you anymore. Ask your brain, ask your heart, ask your loins: *Why do you really, truly want to save money for this thing?*

Remember: no one's watching you, and there's no need to impress anyone. This is your savings goal, so you gotta feel it in your gut. If the real reason you want a Mercedes is: "I wanna flex on that bully Mikayla from second grade who made fun of my mom's car and still watches all my IG Stories"? Fine, I love it—say that. If the real reason you want to buy a one-way ticket to Spain is "I wanna escape my crappy hometown and expand my brain, and also, hot people???" I love it—say that.

Your Why will keep your brain and heart excited to save when the rest of you inevitably gets tired (and you will get tired). But your Why is like an immigrant mother—she will know if you're lying.[10]

When I was saving to Quit Life, there were so many days I wanted to spend my money way more than I wanted to save it. But my Why, my forever-thirst for freedom? That never changed, no matter what kind of day I was having. My Why reminded me exactly what all this financial sweating is for: To Get Free.

Side Hustlin' to Save

(rubs hands) Ah, the side hustle: a saving goal's BFF. When you've got your savings bill, but you're looking at your budget like *hhhwhere*?!, a side hustle can definitely help close that gap. If you've got the privilege of time for a side hustle, all you gotta figure out is: What can I do to earn an extra [insert savings bill] a month?

To start us off, I brought in the big guns: Daniella, creator and author of I Like to Dabble, a side hustle and money resource for creatives and LGBTQ+ folks. (Daniella once had twelve different income streams running at the same freaking time. SO.)

---

10 If you don't have an immigrant mother, pretend it's me; I came from a very good one.

DANIELLA

- THEY/THEM
- FIRST-GEN LATINX
- NONBINARY SOFTWARE ENGINEER
- AWARD-WINNING SIDE HUSTLER

TEXTSPERT

> DANIELLA. I . . . don't have the extra cash to pay my savings bill.

> Should I hustle sideways?! Halp. ↔ 🏃

Heck yeah! 🤘 Side hustles give you options, confidence, resume-building skills, even financial freedom to leave unsafe situations.

> So do I join that random Bo$$babe Product Network that my former middle school classmate is always in my DMs about, or . . .

Heck no. ✋ This is the first thing I warn folks about—people trying to recruit you into an MLM, which stands for Multi-Level Marketing company.

Basically, an MLM = you buy/sell stuff to make money for someone else. Almost all members lose money in an MLM. It's not a side hustle. It's a bad gamble. 🎰

DANGITTTTT.

Okay, but what if I, like . . . barely have any free time?

What if I only have, like, thirty minutes to a few hours per week?

Families are always looking for tutors for specific subjects—dig into family or tutoring Facebook groups in your town or community. You can tutor thirty to sixty minutes per week and set your own schedule.

If you're 💻 digitally creative 💻 and have ~two hours per week, you can make digital downloads to sell on Etsy: art pieces, social media templates, printable planners, stickers on RedBubble . . .

How much 💰💰 can I actually expect to earn with this stuff?

Am I gonna be rolling in it right away, or . . .

That's the thing—you typically set the price for your own side hustle.

Tutors usually charge anywhere from $10 to $50 an hour. For digital art, once you get the hang of listing items, artists can easily earn a few hundred dollars a month.

What if I'm not good at anything??

What if I'm not tryna run a whole business??? 😵

Think of small things you can do easily. Chances are, you are good at something that someone else would pay for.

Brainstorm: Can you help older folks run errands? Can you organize for messy people? Can you do folks' makeup or hair? Can you teach local businesses about social media? 🤔

PS: your "existing network," aka fam and friends, make the best first clients.

Huh. I might make my friends my first vict—I mean, testers.

If you have decent internet access—or can head to your local library to use their tech—you can explore the world of online surveys, reading books/giving reviews, or giving feedback to tech companies.

Keep in mind, tho: you might put in much more time for the pay. ⏱️ 🐌

HAVE A GOOD FREAKIN' TIME SAVING MONEY

Now, we discussed this in our Budgeting chapter—even the fanciest financial plans won't hold up if you don't keep yourself motivated. My solution is simple: life is hard. I don't wanna add harder shiz to it. If I want a new habit to stick, I gotta make it fun. (And honestly, it's hard to feel like all this financial future-building is worth it if it's making you miserable right now.)

So our mission here? Do whatever you can to make saving money fun.

Make Your First Savings Goal Small & Easy

To stick to your savings goals, you've gotta be able to manipulate your brain—hacking into that sweet lil' kick of serotonin that makes you feel body-rolly when you hit a goal. When you're first starting out, you need that kick as quickly as possible.

Instead of having one phat finish line at the end, set up some mini finish lines waaay closer to you, like within a few weeks or a month—kind of like taking bathroom breaks on a long road trip. (Shoutout to my tiny bladder.) If your overall savings goal is $500, but your first mini-goal is $10, I LOVE IT. If that still feels too far off to achieve within two weeks or a month, scoot it down to $5. I STILL LOVE IT. I love it because I'm excited for your smart financial goal-ing and your guaranteed shot. Of. Brain juice.

Remember: You don't get bonus points for stress. You

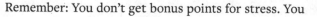

don't need a challenge; you need a win. It's called strategic self psychology, baby. It's called being your own life coach, but cheaper.

Dance It with Me: (Shakes Nonexistent Tatas) Automaaatioooon

You know what's more fun than doing work? Doing no work. You know what's more fun than doing no work? Doing no work, opening up your savings account, and seeing money in there. This is possible thanks to my hot friend, Automation.

You might be able to ask your bank: "Hey, every other Friday, can you automatically transfer $30 from my checking account to my savings account?" Boom, automation. If you are employed, you can ask your employer: "Hey, before you deposit my paycheck into my account, can you put $30 into this separate savings account instead?" BOOM, automation. You save money without having to do a single thing, you take a step out of your money moves, and you remove the temptation to spend before you save. Vacay Berna *loves* No Work.

. . . Or Save Money Manually (and Motivationally)

I do love a manual savings moment—there's nothing more satisfying than smashing that Deposit button—but you've gotta find a way to stay motivated that has already worked for you.

Think of the last time you finished something—a habit, a project, a task. Was it because it was on your phone calendar and you do whatever your phone says? Then stick a recurring "Hit Deposit" invite on your calendar. Was it because somebody was checking your work, so you felt a little pressure to do it? Then ask a Money Friend to text you every other Friday to make sure you /both/ hit Deposit.

I've been in a Saving Money group chat with my friends for years; whenever one of us deposits to our savings, we just send a little 🧧 emoji. Bam—a little shot of manual money motivation for you and everyone else.

Celebrate Every Time You Deposit. I Said Every Time.

Grab your phone, or a piece of paper, or a washable marker and your cat right meow. Make a list of up to ten things that you love to do that are:

$ Free

$ Don't require a lot of equipment or setup

$ Honestly feel kind of luxurious. Like, you almost feel a little guilty doing them.

This is your Yay Me Menu. You can use it whenever you make a deposit or do any other dope money move.

Remember when you were little and you'd go to the dentist, then they'd traumatize you somehow, and then you'd get to pick from the little treasure chest of sugar-free candies and plastic rings? That's what we're doing. Except this time, you get to choose what's in the treasure chest. Whenever you pay your savings bill to yourself, pick something from the Yay Me menu and treat yourself.

Does it feel kind of silly? Good. Just like we said before, this is all about manipulating your brain juices, so tell your ego to chill for now. It's just like the habit stacking we discussed in chapter 2: if you pair *saving money* with *something you actually really love to do,* your brain will start thinking: "Wait—so, after we do money stuff, we get to do fun stuff? . . . I think I like doing money stuff."[11]

BERNA'S YAY ME MENU

$ Deep conditioning my hair with better food products than I feed myself.

$ Listening to a spooky podcast that'll make me be afraid to pee at night.

$ Watching ten videos in a row from my favorite hip-hop choreographer; attempt choreography; die laughing.

$ Nerdy word games like the *NYT* mini crossword. Hey, I like what I like.

Watch Your Money Grow with a Savings Poster

I love savings posters the way I, a grown woman, love dollar-store pool noodles. I don't care if they look silly—they help me, they delight me, and you can't tell me squat.

A savings poster helps you physically track your savings goals. You print or draw an outline of an object on an actual piece of paper, and you fill in or color a space every single time you make a

---

11 I basically money-trained myself the same way I trained my dog. WE ARE ALL MAMMALS, OKAY, IT'S SCIENCE.

deposit—like those money-raising thermometer posters, but you can design it however you want. The point is to finish your savings goal and fill in that entire poster. It's deeply satisfying, probably because I am a child on the inside—but look, we were all children once. I take my inner child with me on my savings journeys because she knows how to have fun.

You can download free savings posters or make your own, like I did. Sometimes I look forward to coloring my poster more than I look forward to saving the actual money. I did this for my student loans, my move-out-of-my-parents'-house savings, my adopt-a-dog savings, everything. It works and I. Don't. Question it.

Get Really Freakishly Literal with Photoshop

Some people do vision boards. I do vision-Photoshop.

It's like this: when I dreamed of studying abroad in Italy, I had a graphic design friend do her thing so it looked like I was jumping in a specific town square in Milan. Guess where I studied abroad for five months—and guess where I took my very first "MAMA, I MADE IT" picture? Uh-huh.

When I dreamed of working at *Seventeen* magazine, I hit the

Googles, found a picture of a celeb sitting at the *Seventeen* offices in New York, and click-clickity-clack—I stuck my head on top of their body. Creepy, absolutely, but guess who offered me a job during finals week of senior year? Uh-HUH.

Now, I personally do not believe in the woo-woo that says doing only this will magically manifest Your Thing. You gotta do all the work with it. But staring at these images every day really kept my priorities straight. I stick these pics where I'll always see them—bathroom mirror, phone wallpaper, laptop desktop, even on my wallet and my credit cards. Every time I've done this, I've stayed more focused on my savings goals, and so far, every one of those low-key-freaky picture-dreams have come true.

Don't Do This Shiz Alone

Oop, she's gonna bang her Money Friends drum again! Because even when I had my comfortable income, my hella-detailed savings goal, my debt posters, and automations up to my overly plucked eyebrows—life still happened. I still got distracted, still got discouraged, still blamed myself into a shame spiral. I was missing one important element: OTHER. PEOPLE. I'd argue that bringing Money Friends along your savings journey is the most important element of the whole trip, if only because it just makes it more fun.

Some Hot Friends Who Save Money ideas:

$ Put a call out and recruit a friend/friends who are saving up for a similar goal.

$ Start a betting pool with your chosen financial family to see who can save the most money in a month.

- $ Hold a biweekly Savings Hang where everyone deposits to their savings before celebrating for the night.
- $ Designate your most disciplined (Virgo?) friend to be your Emergency Savings contact—aka the person you text to talk you down from unnecessary purchases.

Preplan for the Surprise-Money Moments

If you look closely, there are these recurring moments in life where you can usually expect a little bump of extra money—a holiday, a birthday, a bonus, a tax refund. Old You might've been tempted to spend it on Whatever, but now that you're a bad bi$h with a savings goal, you can plan ahead. Every extra dollar you put toward your savings goal means your dream can happen a little sooner. So map out those surprise-money moments now, and plan in advance to deposit it into your savings.

Every year, the tax refund I usually get in April goes straight to my Holiday Savings Fund. I love myself every November, because when everybody else is complaining about how expensive the holidays are, I'm chillin. I'm like, Past Me gave Present Me a whole allowance. Past Me had Present Me's back.

WHAT SHOULD I SAVE FOR?

I'm putting on my Responsible Money Auntie hat: I think your first savings goal should be an Emergency Savings. I know, it's not as sexy as a Santorini 'n' Bikini savings, but in a lot of ways, it's actually the most exciting thing you could ever save for.

An **Emergency Savings** is a chunk of money you save for when life just happens at you, expensively. I'm talking true life-threatening, survival-level stuff. Maybe you get hurt and suddenly need to pay for medical bills. Maybe you lose your job and need to keep yourself or your family afloat for a while. I don't know about y'all, but when I find myself broke and in the middle of an emergency, my financial anxiety is at an all-time high. So, having money that I know always has my back just in case life roundkicks me in the face? That's the ultimate expression of financial self-care.

I wasn't all that motivated to build my Oh Sh*t Savings at first, but seeing that first $500 in my account when I was twenty-five? I had never seen that much money in my savings account at one time. I didn't realize how much financial stress I was carrying around, every freaking day, until I saw that first $500. That heavy anxiety backpack I'd gotten kinda used to carrying around finally inched off my shoulders a little bit. And with every Oh Sh*t dollar saved, I felt lighter; I could make other purchases with less guilt.

Beyond that, an Emergency Savings can literally keep you safe, emotionally and physically. With a funded Emergency Savings, you have the power to:

$ Leave a terrible job and keep yourself afloat while finding a new one.

$ Leave an abusive relationship or family situation, find safer housing, and rebuild your independence.

$ Pay for mental health resources when you need emotional support.

$ Pay for crucial medication to help feel stable during hard times.

An emergency fund can be freedom to move—move away from harm and/or toward happiness, too. Either way, I want you to have all the options.

How Much Should You Have in an Emergency Savings?

All right. The "experts" say that you "should" have three to six months of living expenses in an Emergency Savings. Remember your one-month Life Bill, from Budgeting chapter 2? It's your absolute essential Life Bill, multiplied by however many months feels best to you.

The problem? That number is often really friggin' hard to get to, and it takes the average-paid American decades to save that much because—duh—cost of living keeps creeping up, but our wages don't. This is the part that we can't Tips 'n' Tricks our way out of. There is only so much us working-normal-folk can do when the wages we're given don't keep up with the world's demands.

But if you've got cash flow, don't feel like you have to hit a specific number. Think of what would make you feel secure for your specific circumstances. If you've got a steady job in a stable industry, you could easily find a new job if you become unemployed, you're relatively healthy, and you're not supporting anyone else? Try starting at one month's worth of cash and build up to three. You might want to shoot for six months and beyond if your industry or income is less predictable, you'd have a hard time finding a new job, or if other folks rely on your paychecks.

Whatever goal you set, make your Emergency Savings your first savings priority; the fun stuff is much more fun to save for when you know you've got the serious stuff covered.

What Is a Sinking Fund?

You might hear folks talk about a **sinking fund**—and no, it's not "money for when you feel like you're sinking, like, in life," which is what I thought. The name comes from the corporate world; big companies have them, and us normal humans basically stole the concept and applied it to our cute lil' lives.

A sinking fund is a super-smart money-saving strategy. It's basically when you save money in any account, usually a little at a time, for different things you know you'll spend money on in the future.

Folks often set up sinking funds for random-but-typical life stuff, like car repairs or house expenses—things that pop up every now and then, because Life, but not often enough to get their own space in your monthly budget, and they aren't urgent enough to crack open your beloved Emergency Savings.

You can create separate sinking funds for whatever you want, but some smart examples:

$ Random car repairs (cause the car always needs something)

$ Random house stuff (cause your living space always needs something)

$ Random pet things (cause your dog is always street-eating something)

$ Birthdays, weddings, holidays, celebrations (cause someone's always expensively celebrating something)

You could include sinking funds in your monthly budgeting—when you get your paycheck, you can sprinkle money into each of your sinking funds according to what you need most.

Then, when these random-but-typical things come up—say, your car's brake light got cracked by an overexcited golfer—you're already prepared. No need to dip into your Emergency Savings or snip any part of your budget. Your "Beep Beep Problems" sinking fund (or whatever you nickname your account) got you.

OPEN MIC

To be honest, the concept of saving money didn't really sink in for me—or sound all that interesting—until I started talking to other folks about their savings goals. Mm, the inspiration, the flavor.

To get our savings brains sizzling, lemme pass the mic to some folks from my hometown (!!!). I talked to students from the Center of Innovative Practices through Hip Hop & Education Research (CIPHER) Program, a cultural education program between the Katipunan Filipinx club at the College of San Mateo and Skyline College that helps students of color reach their full potential.

I asked these Money Friends: What are your specific savings goals, either short- or long-term?

🎤 "My short-term savings goal is to buy a car, so I can have more freedom in where I can work and what I can do. For example, if I found a job that pays well for students, but is far from where I live, I actually have a chance to work there. My long-term savings goal is to have my own apartment or house." —Lyell P.

🎤 "My short-term goal would definitely be to pay off student loans because I want to become a marriage and family therapist without the weight of loans on my shoulders. My long-term saving goals would be to save for a house for my family and hopefully start my own practice." —Megan Lauren B.

🎤 "Short-term, I'm saving up at least $13k on just moving out to an apartment, and for a car. Long-term, I'm trying my best right now to learn about basic investing so that I have a cushion for me and my future family. I want to teach my kids or my younger family about independence through a healthy money mentality; it can be a tool and a goal." —Angeli O.

🎤 "Honestly, my savings can feel unpredictable because I'm at an age where I want to go on trips and splurge on stupid things. It's hard to save up when I just want to have fun in my twenties. But my long-term goal is to save up enough to put my family in their own home and live comfortably without the everyday stress of not having enough." —Kaylene B.

What About Saving for College?

If you or your fam are trying to save money for college in advance, you're going to want to look into a 529 Plan. A 529 Plan is a special type of saving and investing account specifically for education.[12]

A 529 account acts like a savings account—many banks offer them, anyone eighteen or older can open one, and you can deposit money into it at any time—but instead of your dollars just sitting there like a savings account, your money actually gets invested, which means it will grow as time goes on. (Way more on investing in chapter 6.)

Unlike some investments, when you withdraw that money to spend on school, you don't have to pay taxes on it. And it's not limited to college, either—it can be spent on private elementary and high school education, too. Having a 529 Plan is like supercharging your money specifically for school.

The catch is: you can only spend that money on things directly related to your education. We're talking tuition, books, housing—and not new fits for campus. If you break the specific rules of your 529 Plan, you may have to pay penalties and taxes.

If you decide it's right for you, a 529 account is yet another way to give the gift of freedom to your Future Self. (Literally. You can ask people to contribute to your 529 instead of birthday or grad gifts.) With your education funds covered, you're free to focus better on the path in front of you.

---

12 The 529 Plan gets its truly stale name from the IRS's Tax Code, which we'll talk more about in the next chapter. Spoiler alert: It's thrilling. Spoiler alert: Sarcasm.

Saving for Your Hell-Yes

Saving money for our Quit Life Year felt a little like the world's longest road trip. I just wanted to get to the destination and take off my bra, but all these little road bumps kept coming up in the form of Tempting Purchases and Life. I needed to be equipped with the right tools. Bigger paychecks were my first priority, followed by a ridiculously specific savings goal, and then that final tank of gas that got me there: having fun and recruiting some co-pilots along the way.

But you know what truly got me to keep saving money when I didn't want to or felt like I couldn't? I realized that the most important thing in the world to me, more important than anything you could stick in an online cart, was freedom. Every dollar saved got me more free.

Once I saw my savings goal this way, my attitude and energy around saving money changed completely.

I stopped saying, "Oh, I can't do that, I have to save money."

I started saying, "Y'know what I want more than that? A plane ticket."

I stopped saying "That music festival costs $150? Wish I could, but I have to save."

I started saying, "Which would I rather do: spend a sweaty-a$$ weekend bleeding money and probably other fluids while pretending I had a good time or put $150 toward my dream life?" (Y'all, I just don't have a Coachella-ish bone in my body.)

When your savings goal is aligned with the stuff you truly want in life, saying no won't feel like saying no. Every deposit is a yes to your Future Self. Every deposit is a step toward your definition of freedom.

And when you find yourself sleeping on a Jurassic Park–esque beach on the easternmost tip of New Zealand, in a tent attached to a car you named Big Tuna, listening to the Singaporean backpackers in the next tent doing an acoustic cover of "My Girl" (all true), you won't be thinking about all those times you "missed out" and said no. You'll be thanking yourself for every time you hit Deposit, for every dollar you sent to your Future Self who worked so freaking hard for this moment.

You'll be thinking: Yes, yes, full-body yes.

WAIT, WHAT?

It might seem like a long road to the savings goal of your dreams, but as always: I gotchu.

How to start (and stick to) saving money:

$ Before anything, check to make sure you're earning more than what you need to survive every month. You cannot save if you spend more than you earn. (Scoot back to our budgeting lessons in chapter 2 to figure that out!)

$ Build your hella-specific savings goal, identifying your Who, What, Where, When, How, and—most importantly—that all-motivating Why. (Page 113)

$ Pick your three favorite Make-It-Fun things to incorporate into your savings journey—any combo of small goals, automation, celebrating your deposits, surprise money moments, or visual trackers. (Page 121)

$ In addition to your Fun Things, make sure Money Friends are involved. What parts of your plan make you the most nervous, and how can your Money Friends support you?

$ Peruse the different types of savings goals, from emergency funds to college savings to sinking funds, and choose your best target. (Page 128)

5

HELLA PREPARED
(AKA CREDIT CARDS AND STUDENT LOANS)

clears throat, straightens out papers

Although the Danish fairy tale "The Little Mermaid" was written by Hans Christian Andersen in 1837, our boy Hans must've had access to a hot tub time machine. Because the entire story is actually a cautionary tale about having hella student debt under twenty-first century, late-capitalism America. In this essay I will—

No, but seriously: if you think about it, there are a lot of freaky parallels between our fave lil' mermaid simp, and Young Me debating whether going to college is worth diving into all that debt.

We both dreamed about being Part of a World beyond our own.

We were both convinced by evil powers that we need to make a huge sacrifice to get what we want.

And we both felt played when we realized the sacrifice was

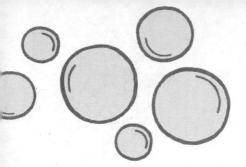

more expensive than we initially understood.

It's painful to think that when I was seventeen, my family and I signed up for debt we didn't understand because that's what we thought we were was supposed to do. As many fellow first-gens can attest to, I felt like the whole reason I was even born was to become a supporting character in my parents' Disney movie titled *The American Dream*.

I was supposed to get good grades. Good grades were supposed to get me into a good college. And a good college was supposed to lead to a high-paying job and self-actualization and clear skin. Then any debt will eventually work itself out, somehow, idk, it's probably in the student loan fine print somewhere. There's gotta be a happy ending, right—why else would they let young people borrow so much money?

But, like nearly 80% of Americans, I found myself wandering Adultland after graduation, feeling like I was drowning in a sea of debt. It took years of confusion and self-education to learn two important things about institutions like the American debt system:

1. They force lower-income, often-marginalized, already-struggling folks into deeper cycles of debt in order to participate.

2. At the end of the day, these institutions are for-profit businesses. They are not motivated by treating people right; they are motivated by money. Period.

But as much as I want to scream "Screw debt, avoid it at all costs," the majority of lower- to middle-class working folks are still underpaid. The cost of living has increased nearly everywhere in the last decade. Survival is expensive. Debt is often our only option to stay afloat in this system where we did not make the rules.

When we're empowered with the right knowledge, debt can unlock incredible opportunities. Debt lets us breathe when we're faced with sudden financial emergencies. (Imagine if we couldn't enter an emergency room unless we coughed up the cash for the $10,000 bill?) Debt allows us to afford major new privileges that our families couldn't access before. (Who has $50,000 sitting around to just hand to a university for potentially life-changing education?)

But we can't dive blindly into debt. We gotta arm ourselves with knowledge so that debt becomes a tool and not a burden. You can learn the rules of this system so you can navigate it without getting chomped. You can use debt to get the things you want without cutting your freakin' fins off.

(Also, Ariel, girl: a mediocre cis-het white sea-boi you saw from afar for two seconds? Girl.)

Maybe you don't have debt yet, but you're wondering how to get what you want without selling your soul. Maybe you've already made your devil debt deals and you're out on land, feeling fin-less and voiceless and helpless.

Either way? We're swimming into these waters together.

OPEN MIC

Have you ever been at a pool party where everyone is standing around in their tasteful cover-ups, too shy to be the first one to dive in? Ten times outta ten, I will be That Person who cannonballs into the water first, and then everyone else feels comfortable enough to jump, too.

Allow me to use that deeply scientific phenomenon to start cracking our shame around debt. To get us started, I asked my Money Friends to answer this simple yet weirdly taboo Q:

How much debt do you have?[13]

🎤 "Carey, transracial adoptee, I grew up hella privileged as a member of a white family but still ended up with $17k in credit card debt, because no one—not even my accountant mother—taught me about credit."

🎤 "My name is Chrismichael, he/him pronouns. I am a second-generation New Yuerikan, and I have $25,000 in student loan debt, primarily because I got tunnel vision at eighteen trying to decide my future and not financially stress out my single mom. Writing this gave me heart palpitations."

🎤 "Nikita (she/her), Black + Filipina, first-gen college grad and daughter of Filipina immigrant. I currently have $28k in student loan debt—mama didn't have

---

13 PS: When I asked this on my IG, over 500 people jumped in and shared their debt. HELLO.

advice on that, cuz she didn't know any better and neither did I when I signed the paperwork lol 😵"

🎤 "Whew, okay. Hi, my name is Rebecca (she/her). I am a white, newly graduated veterinarian with $226,000 of student loans. I have the average debt for a veterinarian—only because that average is skewed DOWN by the lucky few who have parents to pay for it all."

🎤 "Helloo! I'm Juniper, they/them trans-nonbinary, and I have $112k in student loans because I'm a teacher with a masters, just under $1k in credit card debt, bc I've been doing the paycheck to paycheck thing lately, and a $10k car loan because my old car needed more help than I could give her 😌."

Reading these stories makes me deep-inhale with pride. I asked folks to share their identities alongside their debt because I wanted y'all to know: people exactly like you are carrying debt just like yours. Debt is often a silent burden that we feel like we're carrying alone, but in reality, you are in the struggle with so many other folks.

And most importantly? Debt does not encompass our entire identity, financial or otherwise. We are so much more than the financial choices we (are often forced to) make.

INTEREST, BUT MAKE IT TERRIBLE

deep inhale Before we really dig into debt—remember interest, from the Savings chapter? Understanding interest is crucial to understanding how debt works (and hurts), but unlike with savings interest, debt interest is much less delightful.

Just to review: we love savings interest. It adds a percentage of money to our savings accounts for basically no reason.

Now, when it comes to debt? Debt interest is savings interest's evil twin. They're honestly out here to watch the world burn. Savings interest wants to give you money; debt interest wants to make you pay more money.

SAVINGS INTEREST = YOU GET FREE MONEY!

Debt interest adds a percentage of money to what you already owe.

So if a credit card company says, "You get a 10% interest rate on our credit card!" It basically means: "If you don't pay back the entire amount you owe by the end of the month, we're calculating 10% of what you owe and adding it to what you owe. Rudely. As a penalty."

Why the hell does this evil interest twin even exist? (*whispers* Capitalism.) Credit card and loan companies are businesses. Which means their whole purpose is to, what? Make money. Interest makes it so that the company makes a profit when you can't pay your debts off right away. (We'll learn more about how debt interest works in a bit.)

Seems unfair, right? Good—you're

DEBT INTEREST = YOU OWE MORE

gettin' it. Sit your angry self next to mine and channel that rage while we learn about the two most common types of debt: credit cards and student loans.

CREDIT CARDS

If you asked me what I had for breakfast two days ago? Couldn't tell you. But can I remember the exact scene when I signed up for my first credit card? Yup—that's a financial core memory.

A Big Bank You Know had set up a table along a walkway at my university. I knew that a credit card could give me access to money I didn't have—amazing news for a broke college student—but you know  what ultimately got me to hand over my Social Security Number? The fact that they were offering a free sweater when you sign up. One. One free sweater.

That's partially why I was so ashamed of my credit card debt: it was so easy to get into, but so hard to get rid of. I had no idea how common this type of debt was. According to a 2021 study by Lending Tree:

$ 47.6% of people under the age of thirty-five have credit card debt—with an average total balance of $3,660. (This is where I'd be standing at age twenty-five with my $12,000 of credit card debt going "THAT'S CUTE.")

$ College-educated folks have the highest credit card debt, higher than folks with no high school diploma.

$ White families actually report having the highest credit card debt, followed by, uh, "Other" (Asian folks, Indigenous folks, mixed race folks in the house)—and Black families carried the least amount of credit card debt.

$ About 40% of folks with credit card debt only pay the bare minimum monthly payment—and 13% don't make any payments at all.

I wish I could time travel and hip-check myself away from that bank's table, because there's so much I just didn't know that I didn't know. (Y'know?) If I could go back and strip away the muted confusion I felt, here are the questions I would've asked before diving in.

What the Heck Is a Credit Card?

A credit card is literally a plastic card that lets you borrow money from a bank or credit card company. Y'know how a debit card represents how much cash you have sitting in your bank account? A credit card represents how much money you could borrow. But you gotta pay it all back eventually.

How the Heck Does a Credit Card Work?

First off: you gotta be eighteen to open your own credit card, just like a bank account.

It's kind of like getting a job: you submit an application, usually online, to a bank or credit card company, and they decide on a case-by-case basis if they want to give you a credit card. Usually, they'll use your credit report to judge you—more on that in a bit—because these companies only want to lend money to people who they think will pay them back. You either get approved or denied.

If you get approved, the bank or credit card company gives you:

1. A plastic credit card with your name and a buncha numbers on it

2. A credit limit—that's how much you CAN spend

Maybe they give you, say, a $5,000 limit. Dope. You can bring that credit card around with you—to stores, restaurants, shopping online—and spend up to $5,000. You can spend none. You can spend some. Either way, sing it with me: you have to pay it back.

Your **balance** is whatever money you owe on your credit card. If you spent all $5,000 and haven't paid it back, your balance is $5,000. If you spent $5,000 but paid $1,000 back, your balance would be $4,000.[14]

Card number
(The good stuff. Never share this with strangers!)

Expiration date
(Once this date passes, your company will give you a new card. But nothing about your debt or money changes.)

0921 1002 0423 0802

MAGDALENA M.   01/25

Card / Name
(Das you!)

---

14 I think of it like: if I owe any money on a credit card, my finances are "off balance." Once again, we need a meeting with the people naming these things.

Security code (A lil' number they add so it's harder for hackers to steal your information.)

NOTE: Protect these numbers! Always be careful taking or posting pictures of your card.

HOW DOES CREDIT CARD DEBT WORK?

When you spend money on your credit card and don't pay it back, you have credit card debt. If you've spent $400 on one credit card and $200 on another and haven't paid either back? Smash it together: you're $600 in credit card debt.

Now, you don't have to pay all your credit card debt back at once. You could take your time and pay it back little by little with a **monthly payment**. The credit card company will tell you exactly how much you have to pay, at minimum, each month—just like a utility or phone bill—and the idea is that you keep paying that monthly payment until your balance is at $0.

But, *skrrt*, record scratch: thanks to Evil Twin interest, it's not always that simple.

Interest will **compound**—or grow—and add to your credit card debt. The longer you wait, the more the interest will grow—and you're responsible for paying back what you owe plus the interest, too. It's kind of like being in the ocean and wanting to swim to shore, but someone keeps scooting the shoreline farther away from you, inch by inch. Debt interest makes it harder. And harder. To reach. The end.

Let's say you get approved for a credit card with a $1,000 credit limit (woo-hoo!), and it has an APR or annual percentage rate—aka an interest rate—of 20% (. . . 'kay!).

You're like, Dope, now I can afford this weekend in Vegas with my slightly-bougie besties. You end up spending the whole $1,000, because poolside service is mahal as hell.[15]

Let's say a month has gone by after your Vegas trip, and you haven't paid that $1,000 back. While your tan is fading, your credit card debt is doing this:

The time is . . .	You owe . . .	Interest would add on . . .	So now you owe . . .
Month 1	$1,000	$16.57	$1,016.57

Bloop. Credit card companies give you an "annual" interest rate, but interest actually compounds every *day*. The math gets tricky, so I rely on free credit card interest calculators online for estimates. According to NerdWallet's calculator, 20% interest adds an extra $16.57, so your total balance is $1,016.57. You're a little farther out to sea.

The time is . . .	You owe . . .	Interest would add on . . .	So now you owe . . .
Month 1	$1,000	$16.57	$1,016.57
Month 2	$1016.57	$16.84	$1,033.41

See how your interest and your balance grew again?

---

15 Mahal is "expensive" in Tagalog. Mahal also means "love." THERE'S A LESSON HERE.

Skrrt—interest moved that shoreline once again. You started off spending $1,000—but because of interest, your unpaid debt grew to $1033.41. Is that why they call it "drowning in debt"?

MKAY, HEEEEEELP!

That's why only paying the minimum monthly payment doesn't help you get debt-free. Your payment might just pay off the interest you owe, but not actually touch the **principal**, or that original $1,000 pile you owed.

Ah, and don't forget **annual fees**: basically, a membership fee that credit card companies charge you once a year, literally just for having the card. Annual fees can range anywhere from $0 a year, for starter-level credit cards, to $500 a year—the fancier the card (i.e., sick travel perks and benefits), the higher the annual fee. They just throw that fee right onto what you owe.

How Should I Use a Credit Card?

All right, let's come up for air, because credit card debt is not all doom and gloom. Like I mentioned before, credit cards can be a frickin' livesaver if we're experiencing an emergency or truly needing something that we can't afford RIGHT now. We just need to know how to dive in without getting hurt. Here are a few smart strategies you can use to make credit cards werk for you.

Only Put Stuff on Your Credit Card That You Can Already Afford in Cash

Picture me yelling to me in a mirror: AYE. BERNA. Spending money you don't already have is how you got into $12,000 of credit card debt. Get it together. *financial forehead kiss*

Obviously, emergencies happen, and that's the wonderful thing about credit cards: they're there for you if you truly need money, like a scuba diver's backup oxygen tank. But keeping debt on your credit card can sink your credit score (more on this in a few), and as we now know, interest is a jerk.

Make this a hard-stop rule: aside from seriously-for-real emergencies, if you can't afford to pay for something in cash, then you can't afford it. So it shouldn't go on a credit card. Period.

Get Friendly with Secured Credit Cards

Secured credit cards are like credit cards, but with training wheels. It's like a warm-up to an actual credit card. They function exactly like a gift card or a debit card: you load 'em up with cash you already have, and then you spend whatever's on the card.

But unlike a debit card, whatever you do on a secured credit card does count toward your credit score. And usually, secured credit cards don't have an annual fee, either. We'll dive into this in a bit, but just remember for now: starting your credit score/credit history as early as possible is a GOOD THING.

Become an Authorized User

You can ask someone with a credit card—the finance world will call them the "Primary User"—to add you as an Authorized User. It's like becoming their second player in a video game. You can use the card like normal, but the Primary User is still responsible for the monthly bill, so it's on you to work out some type of payback system.

What's dope is, this can kick-start your credit score: if the Primary User is good about paying their bill on time, that good credit behavior boosts *your* credit score. It's like getting an A on a group project even though you didn't do much. (Overachiever resentment has entered the chat.)

The bad thing: if the Primary User messes up and skips a payment or something, that bad stuff shows up on your credit report, too. You're gonna want to pick someone who's already pretty freakin' good about their credit card debt, because their grade becomes your grade.

Keep an Eye on Interest Rates and Fees

At the moment I'm writing this, the average credit card interest rate is anywhere between 14% and 20%. You're gonna want to side-eye any credit card that gives you an interest rate higher than 20%. The better your credit score, the more likely you'll get approved for cards with a lower interest rate and lower fees.

I especially want you to keep an eye on credit cards that offer random, free perks—like those friggin' store-specific cards. They may try to bamboozle you with, "Get

200% off your next purchase if you sign up!" or "We'll literally do your laundry if you get our store card!" Those are the cards that tend to have the 20%+ interest rates and high annual fees, hidden all up in the fine print.

My general rule: if it's a credit deal that sounds too good to be true, sniff the fine print and get ready to run screaming.

Give Your Credit Card One Specific Purpose

Much like your budgeting dollars, I want you to give any credit card you get a specific job. If it's for emergencies only, decide what an "emergency" is right now, and stick to it. When I was new to credit-carding, my "emergency" definition expanded to "this jacket is aggressively cute" and POOF. $12,000 in debt.

If you know you'll be tempted to use it for other reasons, you can:

$ Take a picture of the card information, keep that picture in a secure place, and leave the actual card at home.

$ Use a Sharpie or Post-it on the card and label it something like, "EMERGENCIES ONLY. CASHIER, DO NOT LET HER BUY RANDOM STUFF WITH IT." (I literally did this. It created many fun stranger conversations.)

$ Give the card to a Money Friend who you trust will hold you accountable. If I called my hella-Type-A best friend and yelled "Gimme the card number, FRIED CHICKEN IS AN EMERGENCY," she'd be, like, "NO." Das a GOOD FRIEND.

Wait, So . . . Why Even Use a Credit Card at All?

Mmm, fair q, fair q. There are tons of ways credit cards can become an incredible tool, but my personal favorite feature? Credit card points are life's greatest travel hack.

Remember those school fundraisers where the more you sell, the more points you get, and you could exchange your points for, like, a bootleg scooter? Credit card point systems are like that. But for adults.

When you spend money on certain credit cards, you get points. And instead of knockoff scooters, you can exchange the points for cash, or gift cards, or plane tickets, or nights at a hotel. Typically, you need a higher credit score to get approved for cards with awesome point systems. But when you can get them . . . *hewww.*

This is how my former boo and I could afford to travel for an entire year. We earned more, we saved like mad, and we hoarded credit card points like frickin' squirrels. We racked up over 500,000 credit card points, then used our points to buy nearly all of our plane tickets that whole year—from the US to New Zealand to Bali to Taiwan to Vietnam to Japan and to Korea, usually only paying $30 to $50 in taxes each time.

It's a prime example of making a weird, predatory, usually-terrible system actually work for you. If you're excited about this, search up points-specific resources like The Points Guy, or Google phrases like "credit card churning" to start your rabbit hole descent.

LET'S TALK ABOUT CREDIT SCORES AND CREDIT REPORTS

Quick shoutout to those progressive schools that don't give out grades, because report cards always gave me so much anxiety. Which is why it doesn't bring me joy to tell you . . . we get report cards for our debt. I KNOW.

A **credit report** is basically a report card about how you've handled debt throughout your life. You know how a report card doesn't just show your letter grade—it shows the classes you're taking, passive-aggressive notes from your teachers, stuff like that? Samesies here. A credit report shows your personal information, all the debt you've ever had (including the debts you've already paid off), any late or missing payments, and your **credit score** (your actual "grade"—more on that soon).

It's like a financial permanent record: as soon as you open up your first form of debt, like a credit card or a loan, your credit report starts and follows you for life. A credit report is supposed to show banks and loan companies how good you are (or not) at paying off debt, so they can decide whether to let you borrow money (or not).

I looked into the history of credit reports, and I'll summarize to spare you some of the rage: two white dude engineers made up a credit scoring system so they could sell it to US banks and loan companies. Yup. It was profit motivated. The US is among the few countries that do credit reports.

As much as I wish you could go on Adulting with no credit score—I mean, you could!—a lot of Adult Things will require a **credit check**, which is when they'll look at your credit report. Want a credit card? Credit check. Tryna rent or buy a car or a house? Credit check. Tryna sign up for a new phone plan?

CREDIT CHECK. This made-up system now kinda runs part of our Adulthoods.

(Hold for an *Office*-style deadpan stare at the camera.)

And there isn't even Just One Score! There are three major companies, called **credit bureaus**, who basically put together our credit reports for us: TransUnion, Experian, and Equifax. All three have slightly different ways to calculate your credit score. Because why should this system make any freaking sense?

Reports can look different depending on where you get them, but they hold similar info.

How the Heck Does a Credit Score Work?

Typically a credit score is a number anywhere between 300 and 850. (Another quick stare at camera with my eyes silently yelling, "Who came up with these random rules???") When you make "bad" credit moves, your credit score will typically go down. When you make "good" credit moves, your score scoots up.

A Very Poor or Poor score (anything around 300 to 500) can put a dent in your future-building plans. Lenders see a "low" credit score and see you as a "risky" customer; they get nervous you won't be able to pay them back. You may get denied for loans or credit cards, or you'll get crappier terms and higher fees.

And on the opposite end: a Good, Excellent, or Exceptional credit score (between 600 and 850) tells lenders that you have a history of repaying debt on time, which means you're considered less of a "risk." And that good behavior gets rewarded: folks with high credit scores get approved for the loans and the credit cards with the best interest rates, the lowest fees, and the best extra perks, like travel point rewards systems.

I don't love this game, since we're judged off one crooked mathematical system that doesn't take into account . . . y'know, life? Hard times? Humanity?

But with all that in mind, here are three things you can do to start (and keep!) a cute credit life:

$ **Start your credit history as early (and responsibly) as possible.** Having a long credit history boosts your score, so the sooner you start, the longer your credit gets to grow.

$ **Make payments on time—and if you can't, communicate.** The number one thing that effs with your credit? Late or missed payments. If you are about to miss a payment, it's much better to tell your lender or bank so you can potentially work out some sort of agreement or plan. They might even agree to not report any negative marks to the credit bureaus, but you gotta ask.

$ **Keep your credit card balance to under 15% of your limit.**
You would think that having NO debt is good for your credit
score, right? NAH. (At this point, I am crying at the camera.) Credit bureaus want to see that you are *actively* good
at managing debt but that you don't go overboard. That's
why it could benefit your score to only use a small amount
of your available credit. (Financial experts used to say that
under 30% is good, but I'm an
overachiever, so I basically
just lie to myself: I calculate 10% to 15% of my
credit card limit, and I'm
like "That's your maximum. Dassit.")

GIVE YOURSELF A
SECOND TO COME UP
FOR AIR—DRINK SOME
WATER, STRETCH
YOUR LIMBS, TAKE A
DANCE BREAK—
BEFORE WE DIVE INTO
STUDENT LOANS.

The one shining happy-
thing? You can monitor your
credit report for free with a ton
of websites and apps. I really like Credit Karma and
Credit Sesame, though a lot of banks are offering ways
to monitor your credit without having to sign onto a whole other
thing.

STUDENT LOANS

We've waded through the waters of credit cards, but now we're
going deeper with a different-but-also-super-common kind of
debt. You might've heard a little about student loans—or about
the fact that, as I'm writing this, Americans owe a total of $1.7
trillion in student loans. Stepping into student loan territory can

seem freakin' intimidating.

But you're already in a better position than me; I had zero clue what was going on when I took out my $50,000 of student loans. There is a lot of finance-ese to understand here—the key is to wade through slowly so you can make the best decision for yourself.

What the Heck Are Student Loans?

In the US, getting a college or technical degree after high school can be hella expensive—it can cost anywhere between $1,000 and $100,000 a year. Most of us don't have that kind of money sitting around. So, we borrow that money to pay for school—either from the school itself, from the government, and/or from a private company. The money we borrow is called a **student loan**.

And unless you get a scholarship or can pay full price, the Student Debt Club is a big one: according to a 2019 study by Student Loan Hero, 69% of all US college students took out some type of student loan, often in combination with other types of financial aid. Education is spensy.

How the Heck Do Student Loans Work?

The process usually goes something like this:

$ You get accepted into a school—a college, university, trade school, or other type of secondary education.

$ That school's office of admissions or financial aid office says: "Here's our tuition, aka how much it costs to attend our school. If you can't afford to pay the entire thing, fill out a bunch of forms—which might include the Free Application for Federal Student Aid (FAFSA)—and we'll tell you what your payment options are."

$ Based on what you put in those forms, the school goes: "Here's what we can give you in scholarships and grants" (free money). And/or, "Here's the kind of loans you can take out."

But, much like a credit card: Once you graduate from that school, you gotta start paying it aaaallllllll back. (The Ursula-y student loan providers of the world are rubbing their tentacles together right now.)

According to *Forbes*, the average college student graduates with around $37,693 in debt. I always side-eye this statistic when I see it, thinking about the folks who are well into the $300,000+ debt mark, often because specialized graduate schools, like medicine or law, are Hella. Expensive.

Also like a credit card: for every student loan you take out, you'll usually get a monthly bill to start paying it off sometime after you graduate. And just like credit cards, student loans do show up on your credit report, and whether or not you make your payments on time does affect your credit score.

Student loans gain interest just like credit card debt but with some key differences:

$ Typically, credit card interest rates are 14% to 20%, whereas student loan interest rates tend to be much smaller, like 4% to 7%. Phew.

$ Some student loans won't add on any interest until after you graduate; some loans will start adding interest as soon as you sign up. We'll get into the types of loans in a bit.

All right, lil' warning here: the student loan vocabulary is about to get HEAVY. If you're curious about student loans and really need the info, keep going—but if your brain is skimmin' over the top just learning about debt, hop to page 165!

The Heck Do All These Student Loan Words Mean?

A school will typically offer two types of student loans: federal loans and private loans. And for this part, I want you to think about . . . boat tours. I know. Stick with me.

Taking out a **federal loan**—student loans given by the government—is kind of like buying whale-watching tickets from the company that your hotel recommends. They've been in business for years, they've got tons of availability, and they're a little more dependable. If something goes wrong on your trip, they've got a whole process; there are resources for you to get help.

Getting a **private loan**—student loans given by private organizations or banks—is kiiiind of like signing up for a boat tour from the random scalper-y dude who came up to you while you were just trying to buy souvenir bracelets. It sometimes sounds like they're offering you a good deal; they may have (or claim to have) access to spots that the other tours don't go to. But they're a little more unpredictable, because they've got no regulating boss (like the government) hanging over them—and they're a little more geared toward profiting off of you.

Now, I have a Type-A habit of manically Tripadvisor-stalking any excursion before I go, so I applied that detail-pickin' for us here. Shall we break it down?

	FEDERAL LOANS	PRIVATE LOANS
How do I qualify for one?	You usually just need a high school diploma.	You might be asked for a credit check; you might be required to find a **co-signer**, aka an adult who agrees to pay the loan if you can't.
How does interest work?	**Fixed interest rate**– the interest rate they give you when you sign up is the rate you'll have forever.	**Fixed or variable interest rate**–variable as in the interest rate they give you at sign up can change at any time.
What's this subsidized/ unsubsidized stuff?	Federal loans can either be **subsidized**– meaning the government pays your interest for you, usually until you graduate– or **unsubsidized**, meaning interest starts growing as soon as you take that loan out.	Usually, private loans are **unsubsidized**–no one's helping you with that interest, boo. It's all about the profit over here.
Can I get help with paying it back?	Federal loans are more likely to have repayment plans to help make your payments or interest smaller if you're in financial need.	It totally depends, but most private lenders don't offer the same repayment help as federal loans.

Can I get it forgiven, aka canceled?	Maybe! Some federal programs offer this to folks in certain careers—but these programs are competitive and haven't been successful for most folks. And if our president or government says "We're forgiving $10,000 of everyone's student loans!" they can only forgive federal student loans.	Lol, no. Like I said: Profit, boo. And currently our government does *not* have the power to forgive or cancel private student loans. (But, kinda cute: Some employers will offer employee benefits to repay both private and federal student loans.)
Any other things I should know?	*sends mind waves to current president to cancel 100% of everyone's federal loans already*	Private loans are more likely to offer help to super-specialized groups, like military students, or offer loans for folks with no or low credit.

What Are Some Healthy Ways to Approach Student Loans?

First-gen kids of Asian immigrants might know this song: everything I did from ages, like, five to eighteen, was pointed toward getting into the most competitive, prestigious university possible.

Never once did my family talk about how we would afford it or whether it was truly worth it.

Turns out, getting into your dream school can be expensive as haaayll. And as incredible of an experience as it was, I regret dunking myself into that much debt without knowing how it all worked. I still wonder how my life would've been different if I went to a community or state college and didn't spend the first decade of my adult life drowning in financial stress.

But like we said at the beginning of this chapter: right now, we get to take a breath. We get to pause and weigh out which options feel right for us—which can mean the difference between sink or swim. I can't turn back time, but here are all the things I wish someone said to me before signing my financial life over.

Maybe . . . Don't.

 I mean . . . are student loans worth it? How long does it take to pay off? A 2019 study by Cengage asked 2,500 new graduates how long they think it would take to pay off their student loans, and on average, they thought it would take about six years. (Undergrad me was definitely like, Pfff. Five tops. *winks at journalism degree*)

In reality, it takes Americans an average of twenty-one years to pay off their student loans. Average. None of my financial aid packages ever mentioned that I could be paying off my student loans well into my fifties or sixties.

And we haven't even mentioned the pressure we feel to Just Go to College, even if we have no idea what career we're trying to pursue. Our economy doesn't look kindly on folks who take their time discovering things. (Like, can't we have our life crisis in peace, maybe at home, ideally for free?!)

I know not everyone has the privilege to take time and space to learn about themselves and their world; we've got bills to pay. But if no one has told you yet, let your Financial Auntie Berna tell you now:

$ You don't have to pick the most expensive school.

$ You don't have to take out student loans just to afford the most impressive-sounding option.

No one gave me that permission, so let me give it to YOU.

If Possible, Make Payments While You're Still a Student

Honestly, if you told me this while I was still a student, I would've gladly right-hooked you in the face. Like, with what money? Was I not already struggling with school itself and affording my life— you think I wanted to add more bills on, for funzies? But I had no idea that subsidized loans don't grow interest while you're still a student.

That means: any payments you make while you're still a student goes directly to the principal balance, aka What You Actually Borrowed. When you're still a student, you have a special opportunity to make payments and make your overall loan mountain smaller, therefore making that post-grad interest payment smaller, too. It's like sprint-swimming closer to the shore before a storm comes in. I'm saying: if you've got the resources, it's worth doing.

Make a Financial Aid or Loan Counselor Explain Everything

The number one thing I wish I did—besides, uh, Berna, check your ego and pick a less expensive school? I wish I made the financial aid office folks explain everything to me until I totally understood it. After college, you're largely on your own; you may need to pay a financial advisor to help you understand what to do with your loans. But during college, the school is paying financial aid folks to help you for FREE.

I wish I had pulled up a sleeping bag and held a sleep-in protest till they explained every confusing word in my loans. Here's what I would've asked them:

$ What are the exact differences between all of these loans? Explain it to me using pop cultural references and/or memes, please.

$ What happens with each of these loans if I can't make payments after I graduate?

$ How exactly does interest work with each of these options? Is interest compounded daily, monthly, annually? And what does that even mean?

$ If I was your child, what advice would you give me right now?

Allow me to remind you: student loan debt is a trillion-dollar industry. It got that way because the system is predatory; they let young people sign lifelong financial contracts with no help to truly understand what they're signing. It's almost like . . . they make the rules confusing . . . on purpose? (Capitalism bell goes DING.)

When you are confused, lenders profit—in interest, in late fees, in everything. The more you know about your loans, the less money these lenders can make off you, and the more your Future

Self will be so freaking grateful for protecting your dreams.

So if your confusion is their gain? Your knowledge is their loss. Stick. It. To 'em.

'KAY, I GOT DEBT—NOW, HOW DO I GET OUT OF IT?

If you're already in the deep end of debt and wondering how to swim ashore, I've got some good news: if you read the Savings chapter, you've already got the fundamentals of debt payoff down.

The number one thing that'll help you pay off your debt faster? MORE. MONEY. Just like building a savings goal, you'll need to find extra money in your monthly budget to pay down your debt. And if you don't have extra money to spare from your budget, then you simply can't make big dents in your debt. Sing it with me: the math has to math.

Aside from a solid debt payoff plan, there are only three main levers you can pull to get out of debt:

$ Make more money, or

$ spend less money, or

$ a combination of both.

That's it. It's not sexy, but it's functional; it gets you where you need to go. As a matter of fact, paying off debt is kinda like . . . swimming.

Staying Afloat—AKA Putting Together a Debt Plan

The first thing they teach you in swim school is how to float. How to do the bare minimum to keep your head above water. You can't swim if you can't breathe; you can't pay off debt without more than enough money to survive and a solid plan to organize it all.

Then, they teach you how to involve your legs, arms, your hands—you learn the front crawl, the backstroke, the practical, tactical moves to make your debt-payoff plan go faster and more smoothly.

Only after you've got those down can you get fancy with the flips, the spins, the cannonballs; the extra stuff to make the debt-payoff journey actually fun. (That's my favorite part.)

I'm ready for a dip.

List Out Your Loans by Amount and Interest

I, like most people, hated this part. It's like we think we're gonna turn into stone if we look directly at what we owe. Most people never put all their debt on paper—but when they do, they often find it doesn't feel as bad as they thought it would. So, I want you to list the amounts you owe and their interest rates. And then look at it. With your eyeballs. That's it. That's the step.

If you're tryna choose between focusing on your credit card or student loan debt first? Credit card, for sure. We know that credit card interest rates are typically way higher than student loans, so they're technically the most expensive/punishing type of debt. Keep making all of your minimum student loan payments, of course, but focus on taking down that CC debt first.

Build Your Specific Goals with a Debt Calculator

Hollering back to our saving goal strategy: the internet has free debt calculators, too! Playing around with debt calculators, like the ones on Credit Karma or The Balance or any you'd find on the Googles, truly changed my whole debt-payoff game. I could ask myself: When exactly do I want to be debt-free and why? I could actually see the numbers: How much exactly would I need to pay, above

the minimum each month, to get debt-free by a certain time? Can I find that in my budget, do I need to earn more—or do I change my goal?

This is where your new budgeting and savings moves come into play. You budget to see how much extra you can spare per month. Then, you can literally use the same savings goal strategy from Chapter 4, and build a hella-detailed debt-payoff strategy. Use a debt calculator to help you define your specific debt-payoff goal with a Who, What, Where, When, and Why, like:

I will make payments of $157 to my Sallie Hae Student Loans on the fourth of each month until I am debt-free on September 4, 2035, because I want to quit my job and walk the Lord of the Rings trail in New Zealand.

Snowball, Avalanche, or Shaved Ice?

Once you know how much extra you can put toward your debt each month, you gotta choose: Where are you gonna throw it first? You've got a few well-known payoff strategies to choose from.

You could keep making your minimum payments on all your debts—but you can choose to put extra money toward paying off the smallest debt first. That way, you can pay off that small debt quickly and get an emotional win ASAP, then keep putting that extra money to the next biggest loan. That's known as the **Snowball Method**, because progressing to bigger and bigger loans is like watching a snowball grow as it rolls down a hill.

You could keep making your minimum payments on all your debts—but you can choose to put extra money toward the debt with the highest interest first, so that technically, you're getting rid of your most "expensive" loan faster. That's known as the **Avalanche Method**.

Or? You could get creative and dip into a little of both. I went Snowball on my student loans at first, because I wanted that emotional yes sooner. After that, I switched to Avalanche. Later, if I felt unmotivated and needed a kick start to feel like I was winning again, I'd switch back to Snowballin'. (I call this the **Shaved Iced Method**. I made that up just now.)

It might make *mathematical* sense to save as much money as possible and prioritize the Avalanche Method, especially since credit card debt tends to have way higher interest. Maybe you decide to go Avalanche on your credit cards, and then Snowball on your student loans.

But, if you're like me, your brain doesn't really compute things mathematically, even if it's money. As we discussed in chapter 1, money is incredibly emotional and we tend to attach pretty dark emotions to debt. So, to me, it's not only valid to structure your debt payoff around positive emotions—it's freakin' smart. If the quick Snowball wins are more likely to keep you feeling hyped and on track, it's totally okay to lead with that strategy, too.

Start Swimmin'—Aka Make It Easier

Whew, a moment to body roll here: you've started sketching out your debt-payoff plan! That's a major step—one so many people never get to—so give yourself two seconds minimum for a Yay Me moment. Don't worry. I'll wait.

We good? The next step is to make it as easy as friggin' possible to execute. The easier your process is, the more likely you'll stay consistent with your plan—and consistency is suuuper important when you're paying off debt.

Some ways to smash debt smarter:

Automate That Bad Boy

After messing with the debt calculator and seeing what more-than-minimum monthly payment you feel good with, treat that new monthly payment like a whole new bill in your budget. (I love ignoring the minimum payment email reminders and secretly being like, *Nah. I tell YOU what my payment is.*)

Commit to paying that same amount every month—sprinkling in more if you get a bonus or extra cash—and if you love easy things (me, always), you can set up automatic payments from your bank account to your credit card company or lender. That way, you don't even have to worry about hitting Submit Payment on time every month. Some lenders will even reduce your interest rate over time if you use auto pay. Con. Sis. Ten. Cy.

If You Can, Split Your Payments and Pay Your Bill Twice a Month

Here's the thing: interest on your credit card or student loans doesn't usually come in a lump fee at the end of the month. Interest is often compounded daily—i.e., it's calculated and added on little by little every day. Paying twice a month is like sticking your hand in a stream and interrupting the flow of that interest. You cut down your monthly balance faster, which means you'll be paying less interest that month overall. (Just make sure you're at least paying your minimum monthly fee.)

Communicate 🤝 Consolidate

Now that we're aiming to pay more than the minimum each month, keep an eye out: sometimes lenders will take your extra money and put it toward the interest of another loan, or use it to push back next month's due date. You've gotta tell them exactly where you want the extra money to go. Pick up the dang phone and/or get chatting with your lender: "I will be paying more than the minimum! This is exactly which loan you should put the extra money toward! Please send me confirmation in writing that this change will be made!"

If you can't pay your bill, communicate that directly with your lender, too. They want your money so badly, they are often willing to strike some kind of deal with you—whether that means making your monthly payments smaller, allowing you to skip a payment this month, or deleting a late payment off of your credit history. If you have multiple loans or credit cards, you can also look into **consolidation**—aka, working with a company who can negotiate your loans all into one big loan and one monthly payment. Ideally, your new Frankenstein loan has a lower interest rate than before. But please get clear on the fine print—some companies have hidden fees or surprise interest rate spikes that could leave you in a worse position than before.

Flips 'N' Kicks—Aka Make It Fun

Debt Posters. I Repeat. Debt Posters.

Remember those savings posters we talked about in chapter 4? Same. Inner-kindergartner. Energy. You can get free downloads online or create your own poster that helps you visually track your debt payments. Every time you make a payment, you color in your debt posters.

It's simple. It's psychologically proven and confirmed to help visualize your progress and keep you motivated. But more than that: IT'S HELLA SATISFYING. Did I sometimes make payments solely for the satisfaction of coloring in my little bar, like a toddler? YES. IT WORKED. LET ME LIVE.

Tap into Your Money Friends (But Make It Cultural)

Yup, she's saying it again: community is the super-secret sauce, the cheat code to succeeding in and enjoying almost anything in life. I feel super motivated knowing my ancestors did everything in community, and debt payoff is no exception.

In fact, in Filipino culture, there's something called a paluwagan.

It's basically a group of people who pool their money and rotate helping each other out with savings and debt (and no interest rates involved!).

Is it any coincidence that many other cultures share this same phenomenon—known as a tanda in Latin America, a kou or tano-moshiko in Japan, a cundinas in Mexico, a susu in West Africa and the Caribbean, and so many others? See? Our elders knew all about Money Friends. Tap into your own ancestral knowledge, grab some friends, and give each other that day-to-day debt support.

You could start by:

$ Grabbing a human you know in real life (but who won't be overly forgiving if you feel tempted to spend) and commit to hype-texting each other every time you make a payment.

$ Setting up a betting pool with other folks to see who can pay off their debt faster.

$ Holding monthly payoff parties where you discuss your wins, challenges, and literally hit Submit Payment together (confetti canon optional).

I have no doubt that you could rock your debt-payoff journey all by yourself. But hitting your financial goals with others, rooted in community and culture, drawing strength and energy from others along the way? It's not only working smarter, but working more joyfully, too. Chef's kiss.

Dig into the Debt-Free Community

If you're looking to truly dive into your debt and want more specific community support, lemme blow your mind real quick. Enter: the Debt-Free Community (or the DFC!).

Now, like so many internet movements, the DFC doesn't live on one platform. There are creators all over the Interwebs dedicated solely to documenting their debt journey, and y'all: nobody does financial transparency like the DFC. You'll find creators posting every payment they make, every dollar they save, and every lesson they learn, both anonymously and all-the-way out loud. You'll find folks in the comments who have been following each other's journey for years.

And the best part: you can even find DFC-related meet-ups, events, and conferences near you. It's the ultimate inspiring, compassionate, super-generous community of money nerds like me. (Like us!)

If there's a rabbit hole for you, my friend, search #debtfree community on any platform. Give yourself a few hours, at least, cause it goes deep.

$ TALK MONEY TO ME $
WHAT HAPPENS IF I JUST . . .
DON'T PAY MY DEBT?

Life happens, and sometimes we just can't pay our debts. You'll want to talk to your lender to get your best options, but let's clear up some of the confusing vocab they may throw around:

Deferment: Pausing debt payments because of a *qualifying* financial issue or personal issue. Depending on the type of debt, you may not need to pay interest while on deferment.

Forbearance: Pausing debt payments—but, depending on the type of debt, you may still be responsible for interest while you're in forbearance.

Delinquency: Just a straight-up late monthly payment. Unlike deferment and forbearance, delinquiencies do affect your credit score.

Default: When you've been delinquent or missing payments for a while—usually around 270 days or more. Usually, it means the loan company is so pissed about your late/missing monthly payments, they're making you pay the entire total right now.

Okay. You know how we all have that one Clothes Chair, where we pile our clothes throughout the day? But sometimes, you see it with the lights off and it looks like a monster/serial killer/sleep paralysis dèmon? All you gotta do is flip on the light, and, oh, just clothes. Not a demon. Manageable.

That's how I want you to think about your debt. Forbear it, delinqu-it—but don't ignore it, because that can only make the problem scarier and more stressful. Flip that light on, talk it out with your lender and/or Money Friends, and feel out your options.

Give it a think, discuss this with your group chat, or find me on the Internets and Talk Money To Me: Is now truly the right time to tackle your debt—or could you give yourself a little grace with one of the above options? Do you know someone who has consciously chosen to focus on building wealth instead of paying off debt?

Debt Cramps, aka Burnout

You can have all the right tools to pay off debt, but burnout can still sneak up on you. It's like swimming for too long and getting a cramp. The worst thing that could happen is that you beat yourself up about it and never jump back in the water.

That's why I recruited my girl Aja Dang—known beauty and lifestyle YouTuber who paid off over $200,000 in personal debt— to throw us a lifeline.

AJA DANG

- SHE/HER
- ASIAN AMERICAN TV HOST TURNED LIFESTYLE BLOGGER
- FOUNDER OF MSTRPLN BUDGET PLANNERS
- AVID FAN OF HERSELF

TEXTSPERT

> AJA. ALL THIS DEBT. I'M EXHAUSTY. 😔

> How can I make paying off debt, like . . . actually . . . interesting?

You need to choose the debt-payoff strategy that literally just sounds the most interesting to you.

I'm a very competitive person, so I need to feel like I am succeeding at this as soon as possible.

So paying off the smallest to largest debt got me motivated to keep going. 🏊 🏊

> What if I get tired of my plan? What if I eff up? 😵

You're probably burned out. That's totally normal, but you have to 🎉 celebrate yourself 🎉 along the way and give yourself credit for the amazing thing you're doing.

When I was paying off my debt, I would treat myself to small things every few weeks—laser hair removal for my legs or dinner with my boyfriend, things like that.

I learned pretty quickly that if I don't celebrate my smaller goals, I'll burn out.

😔?! But I'm trying to get rid of this debt ASAP.

Isn't spending 💰 on myself getting in the way of my goal?

When I paid off my first undergraduate loan, I thought I would be really happy. Instead, I started to cry because I realized I wasn't even at the halfway point yet.

When I shared that with my YouTube audience, people told me I was burned out because I'd been sacrificing too much of myself. 😳

We're told that we're supposed to sacrifice everything to get out of debt. But when you do that, you exhaust yourself. I realize that I need to implement those mini goals and 🎉 congratulation moments 🎉 to myself in order to balance out all that sacrifice.

I'm . . . crying 😢

Honestly, same. Paying off your debt is something that many Americans will never do. You deserve to celebrate that. 🍰

Debt payoff can seem like a super-shiny financial goal, but tiny reminder: becoming debt-free doesn't make you better than anyone. It doesn't automatically make you richer, or smarter, or more compassionate; it doesn't guarantee clear pores forever; it doesn't mean you'll never find yourself in deep financial waters ever again.

It *does* mean you can freely move on to your next money dream. And my hope is that, debt or not, you can dive into any financial decision equipped with all the info you need to make the best choice for you.

We can't control every aspect of our debt, just like we can't always control the circumstances that got us into debt in the first place. But we can control what we know, what we consume, and how we leverage our debt. We can work a lil' now to make a plan so that our debt is just one chapter in our larger Money Story. We can ride the waves armed with knowledge, always remembering we have each other to reach out to when we feel like we're drowning.

When we know better, we can plan better, and we can actually give ourselves a chance to thrive in a system that tries to keep us down. We can each swim along a little easier knowing we've got our own backs.

WAIT, WHAT?

It's not easy to shift our mindsets from "BLEGH, DEBT" to "Okay, debt. I see you." But now you've got everything you need to start leveraging debt as a tool instead of a burden. Let's look back at it.

How to start (and keep) a healthy relationship with debt:

$ Get solidly familiar with how interest works with debt (vs. savings)—walk through the credit card scenario on page 147 to see an example.

$ Review all the healthy ways to use a credit card on page 148—and while you're at it, peek again at our tips to boost your credit score on page 155.

$ Get familiar with the different types of student loans on page 160. If you've still got questions, write them all down and reach out to your lender (or financial aid office, if you've got access), right now. Like, right now-right now. (Example Qs on page 164!)

$ Take fifteen minutes to start step one of building your debt-payoff plan—list 'em out by amount and interest. Confronting the problem is half of the work.

$ Pick out two debt-payoff strategy tips or extras that speak to you, starting on page 166. Oh, and text your Money Friend about 'em. Like, right now-right now.

6

HELLA REST
(AKA INVESTING)

deep meditation breath Okay. We made it, y'all—we're nearly at the peak of Financial Freedom Mountain, also known as investing. Take it IN.

It's a big topic, and we're gonna need some motivation. So to start us off, allow me to quote the inspiring words of a fellow first-gen Asian American baddie from the Bay Area—comedian and scholar Ali Wong:

> "*I don't want to work anymore.*
>
> *I wanna lie . . . down.*
>
> *I want to lie the f**k down.*"

Mmm. I love poetry.

That quote is, honestly, the core of my investing philosophy, which might sound a little confusing. After all, so much of the investing world right now is noisy hype: just a mess of Loud (White) Men on the internet, primal screaming every day about shiny new investments and rocket-ship gains. It's like they believe the point of investing is being a better capitalist than anyone in the game.

That's why, before we start to learn about investing, we gotta get our heads on straight. This chapter is a bare-bones investing guide for tired people. For us joyfully lazy folks. For people who want to grow their money while *lying down.*

I don't invest for the approval of feral finance bros, anyway. Dude, I don't even really invest for me. I invest for her.

BLESSED & RESTIN'

This is Bernadette. Bernadette is Future Me. Like, deep Future Me. She's retired, she's tired, she just wants to nap and garden, and I love her. (Bernadette is my actual, full first name, but I'm saving it for when I'm old and have earned that fanciness.)

My favorite financial educator, Tiffany Aliche, aka The Budgetnista, taught me this trick: since investing is all about taking care of Future You, then you should actually envision Future You. Give them a name. Get to know them. Make them real. Who is Future You? Where is Future You in your ideal retired scenario? After their long life of hustling, they've finally stopped working—what are they enjoying now that they never could before?

Now, I'm not a mind reader (just a double Scorpio, which feels close), but I'm guessing you might be like, "Wait. Investing is about retirement? Isn't that hella long from now?! What about all those Finance Dudebros making superyacht-level money overnight on sexier stuff, like crypto?!"

Lemme gently boop your nose with a financial truth: you are way more likely to become a millionaire in your lifetime by slowly (and simply) investing in your retirement, as opposed to getting too hyped too soon on other "exciting," riskier investments. There is absolutely a time and a place to dabble in that stuff, and we cover it later in the chapter—but first, we gotta make sure Future You is taken care of.

There are hella reasons to invest, but I want you to keep Future You on your shoulder as you go. You may see a lot of new concepts and sometimes-confusing finance-ese; you'll need something to remind you why you can't call it quits.

One last thing: investing is a big world with a lot of details, so this chapter definitely won't cover it all. We've only got room to get you started with the basics. You get to choose your own investment path and continue your learning, but remember: investing in you—and all the Future Yous—is always worth the work.

Ready?

$ TALK MONEY TO ME $
IS INVESTING FOR ME?

If you're sitting here wondering, "Should I even invest, tho?" Here's a quick quiz:

$ Are you earning more than enough money to cover your monthly Life Bill? Then yes.

$ You don't have to be debt-free, but do you have a plan for your debt? Then yes.

$ . . . And are you from a marginalized grou— IMMEDIATELY YES.

Fact that you probably already knew: women, femmes, and BIPOC folks have been left out of the investing game for too long. We've got a lot of catching up to do, and the data from a 2020 Pew Research study can back me up:

61% of white households in America invest in stocks—a main player in investing, as we'll learn—compared to only:

53% of "Other" households (lol, shoutout to us AAPI, Native, and Indigenous folks in that vague category)

33.5% of Black households

23% of Latine households

When it comes to retirement—one of the main reasons folks invest—for every $1 a white worker has invested, a Latine worker has 49 cents invested, and a Black worker has 46 cents invested.

Nearly one in five women have nothing invested or saved for retirement—a stat made worse by how 2.3 million women left the workforce during 2020.

Why don't marginalized groups invest more? It's the same song as every chapter so far: a sticky combination of inequitable pay (i.e., we have less to invest), distrust in crappy systems, lack of relatable education, and lack of access to resources that make it easy to invest. It's more important than ever that, for those of us who can afford it, we dig in ASAP and stop missing out on these generational gains.

OKAY. FOREAL. WHAT THE HELL IS INVESTING?

In a sentence? Investing is when you use your money to buy A Thing—like property, art, a piece of a company, anything with value—hoping that The Thing becomes worth more money later. Then, you can sell The Thing and get more money than what you originally paid.

The hope is, the longer you wait, the more money you'll get when you sell it.

For example: Let's say you bought a flowerpot that costs $10. Dope. But a month later, a viral video captures some big Supermodel/Actress/Celebrity Dog Reiki Healer using that exact flowerpot to carry around her teacup poodle. Suddenly everybody and their mama wants that pot. It starts selling out in hardware stores EVERYWHERE. Now, to take advantage of the hype, stores have raised the price from $10 to $15.

So, you decide to sell your hardly used flowerpot on Craigslist for $15. Once someone buys it, not only do you get your $10 back, but you made $5 extra bucks doing basically nothing but waiting.

Boom. You invested $10, but you got back $15.

Investing is the art of buying a thing, letting it sit, and watching your money grow.

WHAT DO YOU MEAN, MY MONEY GROWS? LIKE, BY MAGIC?

This is the part that always trips folks up when we talk investing, and I can't blame them—the concept of money simply ~growing~

seems, uh, scammy. But there are a few basic (and legit!) ways that your invested money can "grow," and the best part? All you gotta do is watch and wait.

Your Invested Money Might Grow Because a Company Does Well

One popular way to invest is to buy a tiny piece of a company—also known as a **stock**. We'll talk more about stocks in a bit, but for now, let's pretend that one piece, or one stock, of the Berna's Blooms company is worth $100 each.

You buy that one piece, or share, of stock for $100, and you are now an owner of one tiny piece of Berna's Blooms.

Now, if that company pops off, sales explode, and the business expands, Berna's Blooms stock prices will rise—let's say to $150 each. That means that your Berna's Blooms stock is now worth $150, too. You sell it, you profit $50. BOOM. GROWTH.

Your Invested Money Might Grow Because "The Market" Grows (?!)

I know—what market? The supermarket? Like, my corner bodega?! I get a little squinty when people start throwing this word around, so it's time to holler at a Textpert—this time, my hilarious friend and investing educator, Amanda Holden, aka Dumpster Doggy. She quit working in investment management because helping rich men get richer made her want to die inside. You know she's good peoples.

AMANDA HOLDEN

- SHE/HER
- ALIAS: DUMPSTER DOGGY
- AWARD-WINNING INVESTING EXPERT
- TEACHER/CLOWN

TEXTSPERT

> Amanda, my wealthy love . . .

> what in the Crab Cake Special is "the market"?

> I'm tired of acting like I understand. 🙄

Honestly, ~market~ is a weird word that investing folks love to throw around to sound cool. 😎

It can mean so many different things, but usually, people are talking about the US or global stock market—aka literally just whether or not people are buying investments. 🏦

> Is the market . . . like . . . a real place?

Nnnnno. It's a floaty concept thing. It's like when people say "society," like, "society is so messed up." Society isn't a place; it's the way things around us are.

In general, when people say "the market is up," it means people are buying investments and prices are rising. 📈

When they say "the market is down," it means people aren't buying investments, and prices are going lower. 🖼

Someone could be like, "blah blah, the sneaker market!" ➡️ Talking about how much sneakers are these days, and whether or not people are buying sneakers. 👟 Again: weird word.

Wow. Thanks. I hate it.

So, okay: the market is a nebulous thing, and prices can go up and down but a little birdie (. . . Google) told me that it's good to invest because "the market grows."

The heck does THAT mean?

Generally, in the history of the universe, most companies tend to grow bigger over time instead of smaller. 🖼

That means their stock prices tend to grow bigger, so "the market" as a whole does, too. It just means the companies we're invested in typically become worth more money.

If you look at the last hundred years of the stock market, it's been "up"—or growing— about two-thirds of the time, and "down" or falling about a third of the time.

As scary as "market crashes" seem, the market definitely does more growing than crashing. 📈📊

And when you say these companies "grow," you mean companies make more stuff, make more money, etc., which makes their stock worth more? 🌱

Yerp. We've seen stock prices go up about 8% to 10% per year 🗣️ ON AVERAGE. 🗣️

I'm yelling because it's not 8% to 10% every year. We've had years where something terrible happens in the world and stock prices totally crash for a while (ahem, Great Depression, the 2008 Recession, COVID) and years where stocks climb way back up and everyone feels rich.

It's a roller coaster, but OVERALL, it goes and grows UP. 📈📈

So basically if I invest with a smart strategy and just . . . STAY invested, don't move my money, wait through the ups and downs, my money will . . . most likely grow 8% to 10% over hella years? By itself?!

YUP. 📈📊🌱

HOW DO YOU LOSE MONEY IN INVESTING?

Ooof—we've gotten to the risky side of investing. No one can truly guarantee how much an investment will grow (or shrink) in the future. "Losing" money in investing means: you sell your investment and you get less back than what you paid.

Remember your $10 flowerpot? Let's pretend you held on to it, but it went out of style, so it's only worth $2. Now, when you sell the flowerpot, you only get $2. Since you bought it for $10, investors would say you technically "lost" the other $8.

Did anyone reach into your pockets and TAKE $8?! Nope. You already spent the $10 on the pot in the beginning. You were just trying to make that $10 back, or ideally, way more. But since you only made $2 back, investors would call it a "loss."

Now, replace that $10 example with, say, a $10,000 or $100,000 investment? Yeah. That's how grown adults end up CRYING. And that's why we only invest money we're willing to lose.

Keep in mind: you can't actually buy anything with your investments until you sell them. If you had a piece of stock that was worth $200, you couldn't roll up to the grocery store and yell "$200 IN FROZEN PIZZAS, PLEASE." You have to sell your stock to someone else, get the $200 cash, and then you can spend that money.

Investments are just floating dollars—all at risk to go up and down at any time, which is totally normal—and it isn't actually cash in your pocket unless you sell 'em.

SO HOW DO I . . . ACTUALLY INVEST?

As mentioned, the first and most important goal of investing is near and dear to my heart. And my butt. Because investing means, one day, I'll get to stop working and sit on it as much as I want.

Ironically, there's a lot to understand before we get to the easy-lazy part. Let's dive into exactly what happens with lay-down-level investing—and to help do that, I'm bringing back Future Me.

O hey, Bernadette.

IF BERNA ONLY SAVED FOR BERNADETTE

Ignore the fact that I'm a whole financial educator now: imagine eighteen-year-old Berna was like, "Investing? Nah. I'll just save little by little, cross my fingers for when I'm older—I'm sure I'll have enough money to live my best life when I want to retire."

She starts working at age eighteen, and she deposits $100 into her retirement savings account every month while living her dope, roller-coaster life. When she hits sixty-five and morphs into Retirement-ready Bernadette, she takes a look at her savings account to see if she can retire. (I used NerdWallet's savings calculator, which used a 0.07% interest rate, to sketch out what it may look like.)[16]

Check out the graph on the next page—that light gray part is the cash she actually saved. Since her money just sat in a savings account for forty-seven years, Berna only earned a total of $994 in interest (those tiny gray parts). Retired Bernadette ends up with $57,444 to live off for the next . . . what, twenty, thirty years?

---

16 In these scenarios, we're pretending we live in an investing world with no fees, just to illustrate how things can grow.

Future Balance
$57,444

Sixty-five-year old Bernadette wanted to chill, but this savings account is only gonna last her . . . what, one year?

Welp, Bernadette just joined the 64% of Americans who don't have enough money to retire, according to a 2019 GOBankingRates survey. And like them, no matter how badly she wants to chill, Bernadette's just gotta keep working.

IF BERNA INVESTED FOR BERNADETTE

Now, let's remix it. Let's pretend eighteen-year-old Berna was like, "All right. Let's just see what happens if I start investing a lil' for my Future Self right now."

Berna starts investing small amounts at first—just $10, $20, then $30 per month. Eventually, she gets a higher-earning job at twenty-five, allowing her to put $100 per month in a retirement investing account while she works. And we'll use that market-growth average that Amanda mentioned: let's pretend the market grows 8% every year, so Berna's investments grow 8% every year, too.

Forty years later, when she hits sixty-five and turns into Bernadette and is ready to quit working, she takes a look at her bank to see if she has enough money to live off her investments and retire.

Future Balance
$353,946

Deeeeym. Huge difference—thanks to that 8% market growth every year, her money compounded over time (more on that in a sec). She only really deposited the amount in dark gray, her "principal" dollars—and all that light gray? Those are her earnings (aka her returns, aka her gains, aka her profits; it's like the same rapper with a thousand names), which she got just by investing and waiting.

Now, currently, the average American needs to hit anywhere between $1.5 and $2 million before the average retirement age of sixty-five to retire comfortably—so Bernadette's got gains, but not enough to retire. So what would happen if Young Berna had turned up the heat and invested, say, $300 per month for forty years?

Future Balance
$1,056,981

Boom. Berna the investor has turned into Bernadette the millionaire, just by investing small, then bigger amounts of money, bit by bit, her whole life. She knew that with savings, her money just sits; but with investing, her money grows and grows and grows.

Bernadette can now stop working and live comfortably; she might live in a condo near the sea and dig into some hobbies she's always wanted to try.

Bernadette's gonna buy some freakin' turntables.

WHAT THE HECK HAPPENED HERE?

Bernadette got to millionaire status thanks to the magic of (angelic choir) **compounding interest.**

It works like this: the longer you let your money tree grow, the more dollars it'll have once you're ready to pick the financial fruit. (HEHEH.)

Let's take that last example and break it all the way down. Let's

 pretend Young Berna first invested $100 on January 1, and that's it. Nothing else for the year. That $100 was the seed to her money tree. And let's pretend the stock market has a decent year and she earned 8% in interest, aka extra money, each year.[17]

---

17 Remember on page 188, Amanda told us that the market generally grows 8% to 10% each year.

At the end of that year, she took a look at her investment and saw that instead of $100, she's got $108.00. How? That 8% interest did its thing.

8% interest of $100 is $8, so add that interest to the $100 starter seed = $108.

Bloop. Berna's money tree grew its first lil' leaf.

The time is . . .	Berna started with . . .	8% interest would give Berna . . .	So now Berna has . . .
Year 1	$100.00	$8.00	$108.00

Now Berna's starting off Year 2 with $108. A year goes by, Berna still does nothing (my favorite), and at the end of the year, she sees that the market did its 8% interest dance again, but on the new balance of $108.

8% of $108.00 is $8.64—slightly more than the $8 we earned after Year 1. Pause: COMPOUND INTEREST HAS ENTERED THE CHAT.

The time is . . .	Berna started with . . .	8% interest would give Berna . . .	So now Berna has . . .
Year 1	$100.00	$8.00	$108.00
Year 2	$108.00	$8.64	$116.64

Didja see what happened there?

$100
$108
$116.64

Since Berna's balance grew slightly bigger—from $100 in Year 1, to $108 in Year 2, her earnings grew slightly bigger, too—she gained $8.00 in Year 1, but $8.64 in Year 2. And she did. Absolutely. Nothing. It grows bigger and bigger on its own. *aggressive twerking* COMPOUNDING.

Add that $8.64 of earnings to the pile, and now you've got $116.64. Run it back, DJ: it's Year 3, and you know this song—when we get to the end of the year, it's been a good one for the market, and Berna sees that her account grew 8% again. 8% of $116.64 is $9.33.

The time is . . .	Berna started with . . .	8% interest would give Berna . . .	So now Berna has . . .
Year 1	$100	$8	$108
Year 2	$108	$8.64	$116.64
Year 3	$116.64	$9.33	$125.97

$100
$108
$116.64
$125.97

Compound interest is that girl. Your money literally grows and grows off itself. All you had to do was plant that seed and wait.

Now, in this breakdown, Young Berna only deposited that first $100 and then watched it grow on its own. But remember: Young Berna became Millionaire Bernadette by adding to her investment account, little over little, every year for hella years. That's how I want us to grow our retirement investments—always adding a little water and fertilizer over time, so our money can grow exponentially faster than ever.

For your own Future You visions, you don't even have to do this math yourself. Just like our savings calculators from chapter 4, you can find a free investment or retirement calculator online. Plug in some numbers, mess around and daydream for your Future Self—it'll tell you your approximate retirement investment goal, and how much you'll need to invest each month to get there.

That's why it's so freakin' key to start investing ASAP, even if you start off hella small: you wanna get that compounding going early. When you're young, you can plant your seed, aka invest your money, earlier than anyone else—which means you get the maximum amount of time for your investments to grow.

OPEN MIC

Two things I hear often when talking to people who are hesitant about investing:

"Investing is only for rich white people."

"Investing feels kinda selfish; if I have extra money, I feel guilty putting it toward just me."

Here's the thing: we gotta break through that mindset in order to bring our entire lineage to the next level. To help us, I passed the mic to some fellow first-gen investors. I asked my money community: Who exactly are you investing for?

🎤 "My Viet parents never talked about money, so I never realized how much we struggled with it. I'm now helping my mom file bankruptcy and go through a divorce, translating with lawyers. Money issues broke up our family. I'm investing because I know my sister and I need to have a different relationship with money for our futures." —Diana N.

🎤 "Investing = growing my wealth = donating to activists and doing social impact projects around the world." —Jackie H.

🎤 "I always learned that all extra money should be going to help our family back in the Philippines. But then I went to college and met people whose parents have been investing for them since they were babies. I know investing is deep, intensive self-care that gives me true freedom to take care of the people around me." —Lizzy B.

🖋 "My dad is an immigrant, and my partner's family are also immigrants. We realized that our families don't have generational wealth. We got serious about investing because we don't think they'll be able to retire, and we want to shoulder some of that burden while also feeling financially stable ourselves." —Vic E.

WHERE THE BLOOP DO I START?

"Starting to invest" used to mean: having enough money (aka $1,000 and up) to open a **brokerage account** (aka a bank account for investing) at an **investing firm** (aka a company that helps you buy investments).

First of all, blegh, and second of all: you can see why plenty of regular, paycheck-to-paycheck folks felt like investing wasn't for them. Who has $1,000 extra bucks they're willing to lose? Why learn all this new information if you don't feel like you belong? There were so many barriers to entry, it was easier to just . . . not.

These days, we've got a few ways to start investing that are so easy, you can do it literally before you finish reading this chapter. But first, we've got a few concepts to break down, so here's how we're gonna do it:

Pretend you're a gardener. Pretend your investments are a garden. And you're out here tryna plant your seeds for your Future

You millionaire life. Here's what we're gonna do:

$ We'll go over the two essential plants you'll find in most gardens: Stocks and Bonds.

$ We'll talk about the low-key pests that'll eat your growth: Taxes and Fees.

$ Then we'll talk about the types of gardens, aka Investment Accounts, you can start.

$ . . . And then we'll talk about the exotic plants: those fancy Extra Investments.

(Note: Much like opening a bank account, you do have to be eighteen or older to start investing your own money. But don't freak—there are a few options for folks under eighteen if you skip to page 210.)

Your Main Plants: Stocks and Bonds

Your first step to investing is opening up the best retirement account for you. But we gotta talk about what the heck happens in those accounts first.

When you put money in a regular savings or checking account, your money just sits as cash. Maybe it earns a tiny *poof* of interest every now and then. When you put money in a retirement investment account, your money is typically used to purchase two types of investments: stocks and/or bonds.

I like to think of them as your two main types of plants in an investing garden.

Stocks: As we mentioned, stocks are lil' pieces of a company that you can buy, and the value of that piece changes according to how well the company is doing.

When you put your money in certain retirement accounts, part of your money could get split up into hundreds, sometimes thousands of different companies' stocks.

And since stock prices can change depending on the perceived success or failure of a company, which no one can predict, stocks are considered more risky. You're more likely to lose big and gain big as they go up and down. I see stocks as a sensitive-to-weather-but-pretty-flowers type of plant.

Bonds: Bonds are mini-loans we give to a company or to the government. Y'know how we talked about student loan debt, and how those lenders make money by taking interest from you? With bonds, you become the lender—you're letting a company or the government borrow your money for now, they promise to give it back in X amount of years, and they pay *you* interest.

Like loans, bonds are mini-contracts—which means you are almost always going to gain certain amount of interest. The interest you could gain isn't as big as, say, the bigger roller-coaster gains (or losses) you could see with stocks, but since bonds are a contract, you're more likely to get your (smoller) gain. That's what makes bonds less sexy, but much less risky and more stable than stocks. It's like the sturdiest, even-I-can't-kill-it type of plant.

In most retirement investing accounts we'll talk about, the whole process of picking and investing in stocks and bonds is totally done for you, almost like a premade garden. Your money isn't usually split 50/50 between stocks and bonds—the younger you are, the more likely your money will be more invested into stocks than bonds (usually more like an 80/20 situation). Why?

Because investment companies believe you can take the risk—if something goes bad with the market, you've got years of investing ahead of you to recover.

As you get older, certain investments will adjust to more bonds, fewer stocks, because you'll be getting closer to retirement age and you'll need that money—you won't have time to risk your cash in any crashes.

Whew! (Rubs hands.) You've got the main plants down. But let's talk about a couple of things that could take a bite out of your bounty.

Your Garden Pests: Taxes and Fees

Unfortunately, investing isn't 100% growth—we typically don't get to keep every dollar we make. Just like the creatures that will inevitably sneak into a garden and steal some fruit, there are two things that will affect our gains:

Taxes: Yup. You generally have to pay taxes on your investments; the government's gotta have their share. The difference between most retirement investment accounts is: Are you paying taxes *before* you put in money or when you take your money out *later*?

We'll talk more about the *before* situation in a bit. But if you invest in something that requires you to pay taxes after you sell it, you'll pay **capital gains taxes.**

Essentially, the IRS goes, "Aye. We know you made money from an investment you just sold, so you gotta give us a percentage of what you made." Real mafia vibes. The percentage usually depends on different factors like how long you've had the investment and your level of income before you retire.

Fees: No matter where you open a retirement account, you'll likely be paying some type of fee. These fees might go to paying the investment firm's operating expenses or paying your investment professionals; you might get charged a transaction fee every time you buy or sell certain investments.

Fees are taken directly from what you earn, and they can range anywhere from 0.10% to 2% of your earnings. It doesn't sound like a lot, but fees can really eat away your gains once your investments get bigger. The higher the fees, the smaller your gains. That's why it's super important to shop around and compare fees when you're choosing where and how to invest.

All right—plants? Check. Pests? Check. Now, we've got some decisions to make about what type of investment garden works best for you (and Future You).

Garden 1: 401(k), aka Get Your Free Money

First thing's first: We gotta hit up all the ways you can invest easily and automatically. In fact, you might already be investing without even knowing it. Are you working a full-time job or a part-time job that you've been at for a while? (If no, skip ahead to Garden 2.)

If yes, then you gotta find out: Is your money already being put in a 401(k), and are you missing out on freakin' free retirement money?

A **401(k)** is a fancy-sounding type of investing retirement account that is named, quite awkwardly, after section number 401(k) in the US Tax Code (basically a super-long book of government tax rules. Truly thrilling). You can usually only get a

YOU   YOUR EMPLOYER

401(k) if an employer offers it to you. What's inside of a 401(k)? It totally depends on how the employer set it up—it could have stocks, bonds, and/or different types of funds, which we'll learn about in a bit.

Investing using a 401(k) is like co-owning a garden with your boss—you work together to decide how things are gonna go. Typically, your employer takes money from your paycheck and puts it straight into your 401(k), *before* paying your taxes—this is also known as a pre-tax contribution. That means you'll have to pay taxes on it later, when you're ready to retire and take money out of your 401(k). In the meantime, that untaxed money keeps growing and growing.

Tons of employers offer 401(k) accounts to their employees, but a lot of employees:

1. Have no idea that parts of their paycheck are automatically going into a 401(k), or

2. Have money sitting in their 401(k) but it isn't actually being invested into stocks or bonds; money is just sitting there (this happened to me!), or

3. Have no idea that their employer offers a "matching" program. If you put, say, 5% of every paycheck into your 401(k), your employer might "match" that contribution and sprinkle that same amount of their *own money* into your 401(k), too. (Why? So you won't leave them. Also, you're worth it.)

. . . Did we all process that? Your employer could be giving you free retirement money AND YOU MAY BE MISSING OUT. So you need to make sure your employer is setting your garden up right.

Holler at your employer and ask:

$ Did y'all give me a 401(k)? (Usually part-time jobs don't, but some do!)

$ Are y'all automatically taking money out of my paycheck to put in my 401(k), and how much?

$ If there's already money in mine, is it actively being invested, or do I need to choose my investments?

$ Are y'all matching contributions? Because I love free money. (Say that verbatim.)

Garden 2: Party Like a Roth-Star

If you're not employed by a company that makes it rain 401(k)s, no worries—your next move should be opening up a Roth IRA with a robo-advisor. (WHAT.)

Let's break that down: A **Roth IRA** is yet another oddly named type of retirement account.[18]

---

18 Roth is the name of the senator who helped create these accounts in the 1950s; IRA stands for Individual Retirement Account. Roth, IRA, if y'all are looking to rebrand with cuter names, my DMs are open.

You don't need an employer to open up a Roth IRA, but you do need to be earning income and paying taxes, like with a part-time job or if you're self-employed. (If you're not working at all, skip to Garden 3.) You put money in your Roth IRA *after* you pay taxes, so that, unlike a 401(k), when you retire and you're ready to take your money out, you don't have to pay any taxes. Contributing after taxes means less money right now to add in and watch grow, but it's all yours when you're ready to take it out. (You do have to make *under* a certain amount of income to put money in a Roth IRA, and this amount changes every year.)

Now, in some types of investing, an actual human gets paid to handpick your investments for you; with a **robo-advisor**, that human is replaced by an algorithm that does basically as good of a job as any human could. And like a good bot, it makes our lives hella easier; robo-advisors typically mean lower fees, since there's no human to pay a salary, and thanks to streamlined websites and apps, contributing to and tracking your Roth IRA can feel as easy as ordering takeout.

When you use a robo-advisor, it's like owning a garden where robots come in and take care of all of your plants for you. You open up a Roth IRA account with an investment firm that uses robo-advisors, then you stick money in there and let the bots invest in stocks and bonds on your behalf. They'll usually take your age into account, and all you need to do is throw post-tax money in there as often as you can. You may be able to set up automatic deposits to your Roth IRA (which we love, because again: lazy investing). And if your investments make **dividends**—i.e., if the companies you invest in make a profit, they give some profit to their investors— robo-advisors can reinvest that money *for* you. (As I'm writing this, you can put up to $6,500 a year in a Roth IRA, but that max amount changes every year.)

If getting Roth-y sounds good to you:

$ Make sure you're working some type of job where you pay taxes, either on your own as a self-employed person or through your employer/your paycheck.

$ Open a Roth IRA account with an investment company that uses robo-advisors and start stickin' money in there. Automate your monthly deposits, no matter how small, and gradually increase your contributions as you see fit. (Don't forget to check those fees!)

$ If you open a Roth IRA without a robo-advisor, be sure to pick your investments—a *lot* of people forget that step, and the money just sits there, not growing.

Garden 3: Are We Having Fun(d) Yet?

If you're trying to invest outside of the standard retirement accounts, things get a bit more DIY. You might open something called a **taxable brokerage account**—an investment bank account not specifically set up for retirement funds, where you can typically get a bit more hands-on with what's inside.

Here's where we'll get to know our Fund Friends: Mutual Funds, Index Funds, and Exchange Traded Funds (ETFs).[19] These

---

19 These Fund Friends can be found in a 401(k) or Roth IRA, too, but I ranked our gardens in order of least effort to most effort. To make Ali Wong proud.

funds are like lil' packages of starter investment plants that you could buy according to your preferences.

Mutual Funds: Mutual funds allow you to make *one* purchase and spread your money over hundreds of different stocks and bonds. That means you technically own little pieces of lots of companies. Dope, right?

The thing is, mutual funds are usually "actively managed" by fund managers—actual, professional investment humans who picks the stocks and bonds for you. And those pros need to get paid. Mutual funds usually charge fees of 1% to 2% of your invested money per year. If you get to boss level and are investing, say, $10,000 a year? That's $200 to your investing humans, even if they picked bad investments and you lost money that year.

Some folks love mutual funds because they want a human to be doing their investing and they don't mind the higher fees. Some folks love a specific type of mutual fund called a Target Date Fund, which automatically changes your stock and bond investments according to when you want to retire.

Index funds: Instead of a human pickin' for you, index funds follow an "index," or a list of companies that were picked to show a snapshot of how the general stock market is doing all at once. Whereas mutual funds are "actively" managed by humans, index funds are "passive"—it's kind of like buying a garden with a lil' of all the most popular plants already in it, so you don't have to choose. There are tons of different indexes, but the Standard & Poor (S&P) 500 is the most popular index and follows 500 large US companies.

I love that index funds fees can be as smol as 0.04%. I love that you can typically set up automatic withdrawals from your bank

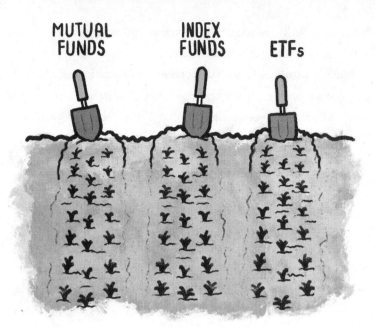

MUTUAL FUNDS   **INDEX FUNDS**   **ETFs**

account to buy index funds without lifting a finger. It's cheaper, it's easier—in terms of lazy investing, I'm a BIG fan.

Exchange Traded Funds, or ETFs: ETFs exist because someone was grumpy about the fact that you can only buy mutual funds once per day. (That grumpy part is unconfirmed, but the rest is true.) An ETF is another type of investment bundle that you can buy and sell on your own, and at basically any time.[20]

What I like about ETFs is that you can choose an ETF that follows a snapshot of the whole stock market, the way an index

---

20 Like an actual gardening store, there are specific trading hours in the US where ~the market~ is open, and you can go online to buy and sell investments — 9:30am to 4pm Eastern Time.

fund does—or, like with mutual funds, you can get real specific and spicy. Both ETFs and mutual funds can spread your money out over stocks that all follow a specific theme or industry you're into—like buying a preset garden of all yellow or all fruit-bearing or all man-eating plants.

You can invest in ETFs or mutual funds that specifically follow tech companies, health care, energy companies, real estate, you name it. With an ETF, you typically don't get all that automated deposit and automatic dividend reinvestment, though; ETFs require a bit more work, and a bit more emotional discipline, since you could be tempted to buy and sell multiple times a day.

If funds sound like your idea of . . . fun (I'm so sorry):

$ Sign up for a brokerage account at the investment company of your choice and pick a fund according to what's important to you. (Spoiler: You can totally invest in a mix of all three types of funds.) I'm gonna be annoying again: pay attention to the fees!

$ Don't overthink it; for beginner investors, the difference between specific ETFs or index funds is SO tiny. I literally Google "Best Index Funds (Current Month) (Current Year)," find the name of those funds on my investment company's website, and test out whatever purchase I can.

$ Put aside money in your budget to invest regularly, and then set up an automatic deposit to your brokerage account. Your investment company may be able to automatically buy more of your fund for you once you've deposited enough. EASY.

As you start planting your investing seeds in whatever strategy speaks to you, here's something to keep in mind. You know how some fancy gardens have all kinds of fruits, flowers, and trees? Having a diverse garden is an investment strategy, too: It's called **diversification**. That's fancy-talk for, "Invest in all kinds of different stuff, so that your money is more protected if one thing tanks."

Your investments could include a combo of stocks and bonds; you could mix in different funds that invest in companies across different industries. You could throw in real estate, cryptocurrency (which we'll get to!), and whatever the latest hot new thing is, too.

My take? As long as your **portfolio**, aka your collection of investments, your whole investing garden, has a plan to cover Future You, then you can go ahead and (responsibly!) plant whatever investments you feel curious about and have the funds for. At the end of the day, the way you grow your wealth is entirely up to you.

What If I'm Under Eighteen?

If you are under eighteen, your move is—sing it with me—custodial accounts.

Like the custodial bank accounts we learned about in chapter 3, a custodial brokerage account is one that an adult needs to open and invest for you. It's like co-gardening with a trusted adult. (It can actually be a great bonding moment if you can do it with someone who is also just learning about investing. Aka, most adults, to be honest.)

This varies by state, but typically at age eighteen or twenty-one, all the money in that account legally gets transferred to your name. You can grab your bag and ride off into the investing/401(k)/Roth/ Fund sunset. Responsibly.

$ TALK MONEY TO ME $
BUT WHAT ABOUT MY (NON-INVESTING) FAMILY?

When I first learned about investing, I felt like I had a guilt cloud following me around. That jerk was constantly whispering, "Hello, what about your parents? Do they know all this stuff? THEY BROUGHT YOU INTO THIS WORLD, AND NOW YOU THINK YOU'RE SOoOoO SMART—"

If you're feeling this, too, lemme put you onto my friend Yanely Espinal, who absolutely lives up to her internet name, Miss Be Helpful:

TEXTSPERT

YANELY ESPINAL:

- SHE/HER
- BROOKLYN-RAISED DAUGHTER OF IMMIGRANTS FROM THE DOMINICAN REPUBLIC
- FORMER TEACHER TURNED FINANCIAL LITERACY WARRIOR
- DIRECTOR OF EDUCATIONAL OUTREACH AT NEXT GEN PERSONAL FINANCE

"If you come from a culture where you don't discuss money, your elders might feel attacked," advises Espinal. "You've gotta be mindful and compassionate when you open the conversation, and the easiest way to do that is to not make investing about them. Make it about someone else."

To get us started, she put together family-friendly scripts so we can stop sweating and start sharing the investment goods:

$ **ON AN EVENT:** "I was thinking about [insert recent family event/drama] and how it affects the family. I want to make sure I'm financially set for the future, but I want to make sure you all are good, too. Is there anything financially in place in case you need to stop working, or can I help set that up?"

$ **ON YOURSELF:** "I just set up a retirement account, and it'll grow so that when I don't want to work anymore, I don't have to worry. Since I'm learning it myself, I have an opportunity to figure out yours, too. What do you think?"

$ **ON . . . ME!** "I saw a video from this girl Berna [lol], and she was talking about a Roth IRA, so I actually opened up one myself. Does anyone in our family have something like that, or any other retirement stuff going on?"

SECRET GARDEN UNLOCKED: EXTRA INVESTING

Got your Future-Me strategy down? Your Bernadette is covered? Savings and debt plan looking cute?

Well then, friend. Welcome to what I like to call: EXTRA INVESTING.

To me, this is like bringing in some exotic birds and imported tropical plants—extra stuff to make your investing garden a little spicier. Here we have

the potential to build wealth faster than your savings account, your hourly wage, or even your retirement account ever could.

Maybe you want to grow extra moolah on the side for a specific goal—car, property, baby, fur baby—and you don't mind takin' on a little risk.

Maybe you want to explore FIRE—the Financial Independence, Retire Early movement—and you're looking to retire waaaay before age sixty-five. (This is a whole community on its own, by the way; FIRE-related books, podcasts, conferences of folks who are turbo-investing way beyond their retirement accounts so they can opt out of the workforce as early as possible.)

Two warnings, though:

$ Many financial experts, including me, say you should *only invest money that you're willing to lose,* since no investment is a 100% guaranteed thing. That is especially true here, because short-term investments can go up and down FAST. You keep your Emergency Savings far away from this place, you hear me?

$ One more time for my folks in the back: Capital. Gains. Tax. She's always over your investing shoulder saying *heeeyyy.* A lot of amateur investors go wild with these extra investments, then get whacked with a capital gains tax bill that they didn't expect. Don't let that be you.

Ready to start? A few things you could dabble in and rabbit-hole on your own:

Stock Picking

Are you super in love with a specific company and want to be part of its growth? You might be able to just straight-up buy their stock. You can only buy stock if a company is public—aka a company that allows us normies to buy stock and become mini-shareholders. You can use most investing firms or apps to buy and sell these stocks.

Many folks keep an eye out for companies they think will get popular and try to buy that company's stock at a lower price now, before they pop off and the price goes up. But, of course, anything can happen to a company—supply chain issues, a bigoted tweet from their founder—and prices can change fast. This is why, if you're looking for more of a sure bet for future (laziness) goals, we prioritize retirement accounts and funds first.

Microinvesting

Microinvesting is exactly how it sounds: investing tiny amounts of money. I'm talkin' cents. You can microinvest from the comfort of your mobile phone via apps—all you need is a bank account to hook up to these apps.

Some apps take bits of your money from your bank account and invest it for you. It might round up all of your purchases to the nearest dollar and invest the change. Or, it might monitor your spending for a while and sneak away a few dollars to invest it for you.

Many investing apps and banks offer something dope called

fractional shares.[21] If you want to invest in Bernify (dream with me here), but you don't have the $150 to buy a whole Bernify share? Many of these apps will let you buy a fraction of Bernify stock for way cheaper, like $5 or $10. Some apps even allow you to see what your friends, celebs, and influencers are microinvesting in. Fintech is obsessed with microinvesting.

Cryptocurrency

Hoooooo. Okay. This is where we step into a "this is moving so fast that by the time you're reading this, things have probably changed significantly" mood, so we're just gonna dip into the absolute basics here.

Cryptocurrency—aka crypto—is like digital money. It's a new form of currency, like the dollar's hotter, cooler cousin who just transferred to your school from . . . space. It's like a stock, in that you can buy crypto and its value can change from day to day. And as of this writing, more and more stores are accepting crypto as payment—like Bitcoin, currently the most popular type of crypto.

The US dollar is controlled by the Federal Reserve and held in banks—and as we learned in our Banking chapter, not everyone can access a bank. Cryptocurrency says eff all that. Cyptocurrency is "decentralized," meaning there's no middleman regulating the value or access to your money. You don't need a bank to use it. You just need the internet to access it, buy it, and store it in digital wallets.

This could be amazing news for folks who can't easily access

---

21 Annoying note: "Stocks" and "shares" are used interchangeably in finance-ese.

banks: undocumented folks, people in regions without a reliable financial system, or straight-up women, in many countries. But, studies are showing that the making of crypto—which involves giant, energy-sucking supercomputers—actually produces major greenhouse gas emissions and contributes (negatively!) to climate change.

As I write this, it's real "early days" for crypto, as the techies like to say—meaning, while crypto is undoubtedly growing in importance, it's a baby compared to the dollar, and anything can happen. Keep an eye on it, tread softly, and always, always, always make sure you have Future You covered first.

Obvious statement alert. Investing is a lot to learn about. And I'm learning it all right alongside you.

Unlike other elements of money that are pretty cut-and-dried (Build a budget! Create a savings plan!), investing is a forever-evolving creature. The rules change; the technology gets wilder; the ways we access, share, and personalize our investments are kinda endless.

And thank goodness for that, because investing is what *truly* builds wealth and breaks cycles of poverty. It's the highest form of financial self-care, because I gotta say: I don't think my ancestors dreamed about me hustling for dollars till I die. That's what they did. Not only are you caring for Future You; you could be changing the money game for your entire lineage. That's a compounded legacy right there. And that's why investing is such a game changer.

When we build long-lasting, ever-growing wealth, we're doing more than surviving. We get resourced, rested, unanxious about the future, and we unlock a different kind of freedom. We get to access the most luxurious, most priceless thing in the world: we get time.

What can you do with all this newly invested time? We're free to do what really matters with your money and your life: change the friggin' world.

MONEY CAN
OBVIOUSLY BUY
HAPPINESS.

WAIT, WHAT?

You know how I keep saying to take your time? I really mean it here—investing is a lifelong journey with so many paths, and the most important thing is to just take one (tiny!) step at a time.

How to grow your way to millionaire status (the lazy way):

$ Take a second to envision Future You. Seriously. Give them a name and sketch out the details of what their Best Retired Life might look like.

$ Get clear on how invested money grows (and how you can lose it), starting on page 184.

$ Hit up a free investing calculator online to estimate your Future You retirement goal (and if you get lost on compounding, review the magic on page 190).

$ Figure out which first investing garden is right for you on page 198—whether that's exploring your 401(k), opening a Roth IRA, or buying funds through a brokerage—and take one baby step to plant your seed.

$ Got a plan for Future You all set? Then dig carefully into one Extra Investing move that sounds cool to you on page 212.

7

HELLA CHANGE
(AKA SAVING THE WORLD WITH YOUR DOLLAR)

Have you ever seen those challenges that are like, "Tell the scariest story possible in one sentence?"

I can do it in one number.

2020.

Let's rewind it back to March 2020, shall we? COVID was getting serious in the US, lockdowns were happening, many folks' income was up in the air, and there was so much fear and panic in our communities.

And my immediate trauma-based response? BE PRODUCTIVE. (I'm still unpacking that one in therapy.) I was itching to do something, especially knowing that so many people in my own community were feeling the financial strain. So, my team and I produced HellaHelpful: an online summit created specifically for and taught exclusively by first-gen and BIPOC folks, available for free. We had classes on everything from saving in a crisis to learning to make money online—we even had a financial yoga class.

I knew we needed this, but I didn't realize how badly. Every class was at max capacity. Our workshops reached over three thousand people worldwide just in that first week. But you know what really shook me? The impact of the incredible community we built.

We had hundreds of folks every day saying: *I've never felt this way about my money before. I feel seen. I feel hopeful for the first time.* People were coming to class after class JUST to feel that togetherness in the Zoom chat. And even though our teachers were sharing their wisdom for free, the community responded with donations to support them, products to give away . . . It was emotional Christmastime for me, y'all.

Organizing that summit is the best thing I've ever done in my career—besides this book—because the effort of nine people ended up helping thousands. Creating the HellaHelpful summit taught me that when we as individuals give our dollar power—and especially when we pool our resources and our knowledge to financially empower others—we can literally change lives. Financial education is so much bigger than what it does to help us as individuals. When we get our money together, *together*, we are collectively empowered to shape the world around us.

And, whew, does this world need shapin'. Every day, we see things we wish we could change, right? Maybe it's a struggle in your community, or a piece of news from the other side of the world that makes you want to flip several tables.

No matter what cause you care about most, I'd bet my entire Roth IRA that that movement could use money to help it along. Every movement needs dollar power. Every movement needs passionate people. And your movement needs you.

So! If you wanna change the world, you've already got the world's most powerful resources literally in your pocket—and I'm not just talking about actual cash, because as we'll learn, you don't need dollars to create change. (Y'like that?)

Before you go savin' the world with your newfound financial powers, there are three important things to keep in mind for maximum impact:

1. **How You Spend Matters.**
2. **How You Give Matters.**
3. **How You Move Together Matters.**

HOW YOU SPEND MATTERS

We all know how hard it can be to keep your budgeted dollars in line—it's like you can't exhale without being tempted to hit Add to Cart. Have you ever seen an online ad that felt so intensely specific to your life, you felt sucked in, almost powerless, like, PLEASE IMMEDIATELY TAKE MY MONEY? That's no coincidence. According to *Ad Age*, in 2020, advertisers spent $278 billion on ads, with nearly half of it going to targeted online ads.

Why the humongous ad spend? Because advertisers, CEOs, and

folks in power know: money is the language of power and influence in this world. So they'll do whatever it takes to convince you to hand your dollar power over. Because without your dollar, a lot of these companies wouldn't exist.

If you think about it, when you are making the decision to buy something, you're holding the dollar—so YOU are the one in power. You get to be the picky bachelor/bachelorette with the rose. And with all that power, we have a responsibility to shift our spending mindset. Every dollar you spend is a vote toward the kind of world you wanna see.

Now, pause here: I don't want you thinking that larger issues like systemic racism or climate change exist because you, as an individual, aren't doing enough or spending the "right" way. There are corporations and individuals out there with truly disproportionate amounts of power and influence over our world—like the ninety companies who are responsible for nearly 75% of greenhouse gas emissions, according to geographer and researcher Richard Heede. And these capitalist structures we are all living in, working in, and actively resisting aren't going anywhere anytime soon.

While we won't be able to change things overnight, there are steps we can all take now to make a difference. We can move toward new systems, we can hold those in power accountable, and we can move our dollars intentionally. All of these efforts have their place in changing the world. Let's zoom it back to you—what you choose to buy and not buy has more power than you think. Because when we normal folk hold back our dollar power, leaders tend to listen.

Do Your Homework (But We Like This Homework)

Enter: financial frickin' resistance. Activists have been teaching us for decades how to make folks in power listen using our dollars. We've seen **boycotts**, which is when many people refuse to buy from a certain brand until the brand gets their act together. We've seen **strikes**, which is when workers refuse to work under unfair conditions and hold back the power they have to make dollars for their boss.

When the pockets dry up, the ears perk up, and history says this is a fact.

Our money power-move	Why it worked
In 1955, the legendary Rosa Parks refused to leave her seat on a racially segregated bus in Montgomery, Alabama—prompting Black folks to boycott the Montgomery bus system for thirteen months.	The national attention got so loud that the US Supreme Court stepped in, officially making bus segregation illegal.
Filipino American labor worker Larry Itliong led the first strike against grape growers in 1965, and asked Californians to stop buying grapes until workers received better pay and safer treatment.	It took five freakin' years of strikes, but it worked—in 1971, growers finally signed a new contract with workers ensuring higher pay and health benefits.

Hundreds of thousands of users deleted Uber when #DeleteUber went viral in 2017, after the ride-service app was accused of siding with President Trump during his travel ban against Muslim people.

Uber had one of its lowest-earning years ever, and its CEO cut ties with President Trump's business council and eventually left the company.

After suffering under unfair working conditions during the COVID pandemic, workers in over forty workplaces, from Kellogg to Twitch, went on strike and refused to work (aka Striketober 2021). And that was after the Great Resignation of 2020, when folks left their jobs in record-breaking numbers amid the strain of the pandemic.

Workers saw wins across the board. For example, after an eleven-week strike, Kellogg's workers in four states reached an agreement with their employees, giving them well-overdue wage increases, cost-of-living adjustments, and better health care and retirement benefits.

Now, it can feel hella overwhelming to try and track a company's do-good record every time you go to buy something. We've gotta get comfortable doing some good ol' internet stalki—I mean, research. (Like, BTS Army investigating every last detail about their fave/bias? Channel that energy.)

So, let's split the work a bit. You start by picking one thing you care about—and based on that, I've drawn up a few questions to start off your search.

If you care about . . .	Then get stalkin' on . . .
Anti-racism	Check the external: Has this company ever perpetuated racism? If so, have they owned up to it and made a point to do better?
	Have they ever actually given resources to an anti-racist cause or backed up their progress with metrics and updates?
	Find their leadership teams, their board of directors: Do they hire BIPOC to top decision-making positions?
Workers being treated fairly	What actual humans made this thing, and in what country?
	Were they treated and paid fairly for where they live?
	Has there been anything in the news or on social about this company treating their employees unfairly?
Rich people doing corrupt stuff	Who's the CEO of this company?
	How does the CEO, or any of the company's leaders, spend their money?
	Have this company's leaders been involved in any horrible scandals?
Saving the planet	What materials are used to make this thing?
	Do those materials harm the planet?
	Does the company make any effort to reduce waste or contribute to organizations that are doing meaningful environmental work?

If you can't find the information you're looking for? Ask.

Hit up your bank, your employer, or any brand you're thinking of giving your money to and say you're looking for clarification: Are you currently invested in private prisons? In women-led businesses? Are you invested in companies that contribute negatively to [issue you care about] or support [community you care about]?

If you do your sleuthing and get that blegh, bad-vibe, financial-ick feeling? That's when we make real moves with our money—we might boycott, or we might divest.

As we learned in our lil' history stop above, to boycott (in the money world) means to refuse to use or buy a product as an expression of protest. It's a non-violent way to flex on problematic companies because again, our dollar is power.

Now, if we want to flex our power by breaking up with a crappy financial institution, like a bank or investment? That's called **divesting.** We can withdraw our funds, sell our investments, and boogie on elsewhere.

I give you full permission to make hella noise as you leave, too. Let the company know why they lost your dollars. Add to the chorus of folks calling them out on social media, and amplify that noise. It's a sad truth of capitalism, but if enough folks make noise, the company might decide that it's simply bad business to keep up their garbage practices. You use their greed for good. Oh—and don't forget to take our Money Friends with you on the way out, too.

Whether you decide to go into super-sleuth mode months before hitting the Buy button, or you're just casually perusing your favorite store, recognizing your dollar power comes down to a few simple questions we can carry anywhere:

Who deserves your dollar? Who do you want to see win? Who do you really want to give your power to?

$ TALK MONEY TO ME $
BUYING ETHICALLY IS COMPLICATED

Now, here's the catch: learning all of these new tools does not mean we go around yelling "Everyone who doesn't spend ethically is a monster!!" This is where things get a liiiiittle nuanced.

If you're focused on your or your family's survival, you don't always have the luxury of choosing between feeding your morals vs. feeding mouths. Sometimes you just need The Thing for the cheapest price possible so you can survive. Being able to shop intentionally is a massive privilege, so we need to be able to sit with the complicated Yes, Ands.

Yes, "fast fashion" is made in sweatshop conditions, and the throwaway quality contributes massively to pollution. *And* sometimes, fast fashion is all we can afford.

Yes, Big Box CEO billionaires go to Mars for funzies while paying their workers minimum wage, without benefits, in dangerous working conditions. *And* sometimes, those Big Box stores are all we can afford.

When we have limited choices, we are not selling out. We are surviving. We have to be able to hold both truths at the same time: intentional spending matters, *and* it's a privilege that not all folks can enjoy.

Give it a think, discuss this with your group chat, or find me on the Internets and Talk Money To Me: Were there times in your life that you or your family could not afford to buy ethically? Are there purchases in your life where you'll always go for the cheapest option, or the most ethical, no matter what?

Buy It with Your Chest

While we work toward a world of fairer wages and equitably distributed wealth, those of us who can afford to spend consciously have an amazing opportunity: we get to use our dollars to help other people win. We don't need to spend numbly or mindlessly anymore—we get to buy stuff with hype. Literally. When I spend with intention, I literally feel like I'm doing a lil' financial booty shake with whatever cause or community I'm supporting.

< Notes

UR DOIN UR BEST UNDER CAPITALISM <3

We can hype up the causes we care about through our everyday purchases. For example, we can choose to buy local produce that doesn't require tons of fuel to truck, unlike the grocery chain brands. We can shift our daily iced matcha habit to the coffee shop that employs formerly incarcerated folks. We can consciously save up a few more dollars for the jeans we know were made by a company that pays their workers fairly.

We can hype up the business owners we wanna see win, too. We can choose to buy specifically from BIPOC and LGBTQIA+

creators; from disabled and neurodiverse creators, and whoever else you're rooting for. Every time I purchase something from a Filipinx-owned business, I'm saying, "I want more Filipinx folks to succeed in this hellscape." (And is it a coincidence that I feel extra hot in my ethically bought drip?!)

And we can apply this same intentional hype to the way we invest, too. You can choose to dig into Socially Responsible Investing, or SRI. SRI is a new-ish investment strategy where you purposely invest in companies or funds that have a positive social impact. There are entire indexes, funds, and even online investing platforms that focus entirely on helping you find SRI-related investments—all-climate-change focused funds, for example, or all-women-led-business funds.

And to take it a step further: we can choose to understand our own privileges, to know how much financial power we have in comparison to folks around us. We can choose to leave good tips for service folks, restaurant staff, and other people who make a living making our lives easier. Instead of spending numbly, we can spend from a place of joy, from a place of "We got each other."

Every dollar you spend is an endorsement, a vote for that community's success, a little piece of hype for that human. Your. Dollar. Matters.

HOW YOU GIVE MATTERS

There's a second way to multiply our financial impact: we can give our money. We can donate. We can use our dollars to tangibly support each other, aka (neon flashing lights come down from the ceiling, microphone appears outta nowhere) COLLECTIVE FINANCIAL CAAAAARE.

WHEN I SAY COMMUNITY, YOU SAY CARE

When I think of collective financial care, I think of the Filipino word kapwa.

Kapwa is at the heart of Filipino culture and activism. The word technically means "fellow human" or "neighbor," but deep down, it really speaks to how each of us is naturally equal to each other, and that all of our experiences—the good, the bad, the systemically oppressive—are interconnected. It means that I am you, and you are me.

Because of that, kapwa is at the heart of my financial activism, too. When I see injustice toward others, I feel connected to their struggle, so when I give my dollars to support them, I don't just feel like it's a one-way transaction. Donating my money means lending my dollar power so that we can all get a lil' more financially free, together. And if you've ever donated money, you know: It feels. Freaking. Good.

How can we make this kind of win-win financial activism a part of our daily life? I wish you could see the smug look on my face, because the answer is my favorite: budgeting, baby.

Budgeting For Justice

Now, see, what I don't want to happen? I don't want you to panic-donate whatever amounts of money whenever a crisis hits. (Which is all the time.)

It's just like our approach to budgeting that we learned in chapter 2: you've gotta create some structure around the way you move your money so that you are always in control. And you gotta always make sure your financial oxygen mask is secured while helping others. To do that, you can—must!—make community care a part of your budget, just like any other part of your life. And the easiest way to do that is to let your budget do the work for you.

Now that you're a pro at doing that monthly budgeting math, you can stick whatever amount of community care into your regular payments, as if you're paying a bill—just like those savings or debt-payoff bills. I like to think of it like: "Whew, I'm grateful for my privileges this month; lemme pass the good energy on to someone in my community to give thanks." Some folks call it their Justice Budget, their Privilege Bill, their Give-Back Bill; I call it my Community Care Funds.

Let's say you did your budgeting dance and found out that you can put aside $10 to donate every month. Some next steps:

$ You can choose a different cause to donate to every month.

$ You can contact your favorite nonprofit and ask if they can set up recurring—fancy word for "repeating"—donations for $10 the same time each month. Some organizations can automatically take that $10 from your account. That way, you don't lift a finger.

$ You can recruit a Money Friend to also be your Community Care Buddy so that 1. you've got a friend to tell once you get that serotonin "I did iiiit" feeling after hitting donating, and 2. you literally double your impact by moving your friends' dollars toward your mission, too.

How much should we donate each month? To answer this, I picked up a couple of questions from author and activist Sonya Renee Taylor to help us think about our relationship to money and our communities. She urges us to ask ourselves:

$ **What do I have?** Get honest about your budget: Am I giving from a place of scarcity, used to having so little and afraid of giving too much? Do I actually have more to give?

$ **What's appropriate to give?** What's the power dynamic between you and the community you're donating to? What privileges have put you in the position to give more? With this in mind, what feels appropriate to you?

What if you've taken a good hard look at your budget and you can only give a tiny amount? You might hear the phrase "every dollar counts" all the time, but it's cliché because it's true.

Giving small amounts is called **microdonating**, and when you

do it consistently, it has a major impact. Small, regular donations are super helpful to nonprofits because they can actually plan for the future, knowing your funds are for sure coming in. If you're more likely to be consistent about a small donation than a bigger, one-time thing, then stick to it. You're giving the extra gift of stability.

This is some critical financial brain jerky to chew on, but ultimately, the only one who can answer those questions is you. It's the same for both social justice and personal finance: our approach has to be flexible and change with the times so you can always adjust your budget to fit the needs of both you and your community.

After your Community Care Funds are budgeted, we can get to the juicy part: deciding how to move those funds the way that feels best for you. You've got two important moves to learn here. There's donating to a charitable organization, and then there's mutual aid.

Donating: Passing the Mic

$471 billion. That's how much Americans donated to charitable organizations in 2020 alone, according to a report by the Giving USA. Folks really wanted a way to help with the buffet of crises happening that year, so they came through and broke records with their wallets.

Donating to a nonprofit can be a powerful way to help create change for so many reasons. You're not just handing money over to an organization—you're helping to equip people who straight-up know more than you, and already know where cash is needed.

Donating is also an incredible way to uplift systematically excluded voices and pass the mic without taking up space and hogging the stage yourself. No need to start a new campaign or movement; you let your money talk for you, turning up the volume for folks who have *been* serving those communities.

Now, when you're donating to a charity or organization, it's usually a one-way relationship—the donor is giving to a recipient, usually through a nonprofit organization with a certain tax status with the IRS. (Pro tip: Donations can often be deducted from your taxes. Keep the receipts or confirmations when you donate to a nonprofit or charitable organization. You can report some donations when you file your taxes, which could lower your tax bill.)

OPEN MIC BOX

When that wave of anti-racism protests popped off in 2020, folks were super eager to throw their money at social causes. The number one donation question that flooded my DMs: Where exactly does my donated money go?

Lemme pass the mic to some nonprofit and social justice folks in my @heyberna online community to tell us what happens when the contributions start rolling in.

- 🎙 "Your donations help us give no-strings-attached cash directly to survivors of intimate partner violence." —FreeFrom

- 🎙 "Your donation buys CSA shares from BIPOC farmers, then food goes to local BIPOC who are food insecure." —Elizabeth for Equitable Giving Circle

- 🎙 "Your donation provides subsidized childcare to low-income families in my hometown of Honolulu, Hawaii." —Dominique for the Leeward YMCA

- 🎙 "Donations pay for trainings to help support women

of color who decide to run for office." —Maggie C. for Emerge America

🎙 "Donations go to team stipends for Slant'd, an Asian American creative collective, which is run entirely by AAPI volunteers." —Krystie Y. for Slant'd Creative

🎙 "Your donation buys period products for people who menstruate and can't afford/access. Small donations help organizations be flexible!" —Emer for Bloody Good Period

Mutual Aid: Sharing the Stage

It used to be that donating to a charitable organization was our go-to answer for giving. But because of, well . . . the world becoming increasingly (gestures wildly), community activists and organizers have taught us a different way to contribute: mutual aid.

I learned about mutual aid from the writings of organizer and educator Mariame Kaba. While donating is often a one-way financial street, mutual aid is a cycle—it's structured so that you could both give and receive continuously. It's based on the belief that everyone has something to give, and everyone has something they need, too. You might donate to a local mutual aid fund that redistributes money across a bunch of resources for a whole community—delivering fresh meals to elderly folks or creating accessible community food pantries—with the idea that *you* can also receive those resources as part of the system. (Important note: You usually can't deduct mutual aid contributions from your taxes.)

Now, how can you move your money to participate in mutual aid? You can go bigger by joining a mutual aid group near you, which are usually hyper-focused on local issues. But one of my favorite methods of mutual aid? You can support someone right in your network, exchanging financial energy 1:1.

Maybe you know an educator on social media who has put labor into teaching you something for free, and in exchange, they invite you to drop something into their CashApp. Maybe you know a health care friend having a rough day who you could Venmo and cover their dinner, knowing they'd trade off and do the same for you when you're going through it.

The practice of mutual aid is all about letting money flow to build a network from which you can give and receive help, either between individuals or inside of a bigger collective, without relying on political structures or leaders. Building our own financial systems to give each other care, freedom, and nurturing in a crisis? That's a frickin' powerful, intimate revolutionary move.

Rule of thumb here: make sure that you're always following folks' boundaries on how, when, or whether to give. Always move according to the relationship you already have—ask them what they need first!—or according to what money channels that person has explicitly offered. (Don't go randomly Venmo-ing your One Asian Friend from High School after seeing an attack against Asian folks on the news, is what I'm saying.)

How Do I Choose Where to Give?

Whether you're giving to an established nonprofit organization, a mutual aid fund, or even a crowdsourced GoFundMe campaign: you gotta stay in control of your money, because unfortunately, not everyone in the club has a pure heart.

Just because it's a nonprofit doesn't automatically mean it's legit—"nonprofit" is simply a tax status an organization can qualify for. To see if they align with your money energy, here are some points to look out for:

$ **What fees do they charge?** You know how sites like GoFundMe make their money? They typically collect donation "fees" every time you donate; that extra bit of money goes to keeping the site running and its employees paid, not to the person in need.

$ **How's this money moving?** Does the organization's page say exactly what the funds will be used for, why, and when? Is the organizer giving consistent updates, responding to comments or questions, and being transparent? Do they say exactly how the money will be transferred?

$ **Who's running this thing?** Sadly, scammers often pop up when a crisis hits, so click around to make sure the person organizing a fundraising campaign is actually the person who needs help. If they're organizing on behalf of someone, see if the connection is clear. A campaign that has the obvious support of directly related family and friends is a campaign we like.

$ TALK MONEY TO ME $
PAY YOUR FRIGGIN' LAND TAX

Maybe you've never heard of Land Tax, but it's picking up steam across the US. Essentially, it's a way of acknowledging with our dollars that every day, non-Indigenous folks like me live on land stolen from Indigenous peoples. (Shoutout to the Native Governance Center for schooling me on this!)

When we pay Land Tax, the funds might go to programs that are working toward returning the land to Indigenous folks, or to other supporting programs, or directly to local Indigenous folks themselves.

You should do your own research and learn about Land Tax directly from Indigenous organizers. This varies from program to program, but typically, anyone can pay Land Tax, at any time, and you choose the amount that fits your budget.

To me, paying Land Tax doesn't mean I check off a "Yay, I Supported Indigenous People" box for the year. It's simply one way of showing respect, and a means of distributing my wealth so that Indigenous folks can get resources they need. Financial community care at its best, my friends.

WE LIVE ON STOLEN LAND

HOW YOU MOVE TOGETHER MATTERS

A little moment to review: As individuals, we can spend consciously, and we can take a step beyond that to give and donate consciously, too. But making all of these moves on your own? That shiz can get overwhelming, and it's easy to feel like your efforts aren't making a difference. So what happens when we party up—when we combine our dollar power with other folks?

Let's zoom it on back to the HellaHelpful summit. My role was The Organizer. It was not my job to be the smartest teacher; I left that up to our six incredible educators. It was not my job to be good at marketing—Joely, our community manager, crushed that—and our giveaways would've fallen apart without Jeffrey, our administrative assistant. And without the community, who were donating funds, creating the vibes in the Zoom, and hyping each other up, we'd have nothing.

It turns out, we were ALL sitting in the same feelings in 2020, waiting for an outlet for our financial fear and anxiety. I had no idea that other folks were waiting for me to fill my role so that they could unlock theirs. That's the true magic of what we now know as financial activism: real change happens when we combine our powers, dollars, and otherwise for good.

To help us understand how powerful we truly are as a collective, I hit up the best person for the job—my good friend Dasha Kennedy, aka @thebrokeblackgirl.

DASHA KENNEDY:

- SHE/HER
- MILLENNIAL FINANCIAL COACH
- OWNER OF THE BROKE BLACK GIRL
- FINANCIAL ACTIVIST

TEXTSPERT

> Dasha, honest question:

> If I spend consciously, and I donate, and, like, I always use paper straws

> Will that, uh, fix the world? 👀👀

Those are all great practices, but remember: the responsibility of "fixing" the world does not lie solely on what *you* do. ☝🏽

Our money helps fund every aspect of the most powerful companies. Those companies manipulate this message by shifting the blame back on individuals.

They make you think that your power is small and useless, when in reality, your power extends far beyond your own dollar.

The real power lies in moving together. 💪🏽💪🏾

But what are we aiming for when we move our dollars together?

Is the goal to just make everyone . . . more rich?

Some folks believe that financial activism means if we can make everyone rich, then all of our problems will go away. Absolutely not.

Massive wealth accumulation produces wealth inequality, which upholds the cycle of wealth hoarding, resulting in poverty.

Financial activism means fighting to provide equitable economic opportunities to purposely ignored communities, mostly Black and brown women and children.

Big emphasis on the word ✨ equitable ✨; it matters.

Hard agree. Because Equal = giving everyone the SAME resources.

Equitable = giving resources based on everyone's NEEDS. 🧠

So, um. How . . . How do we . . . start.

Can I just repost a social justice meme, or—

> You can use social media to amplify your voice, but not as a replacement for your grassroots work.

> Your first step: Listen to the folks around you. There is no one better qualified to tell you about inequality than the people most impacted by it. Your community will tell you what they need.

> Listen to their needs, leverage your voices, and flip the f*&%in' table as a collective. 💪🗡️

Ahem. I don't know about y'all, but when Dasha says community and collective, the same song kept playing in my head. One that we should be pretty familiar with at this point.

Yup. It's, like, Ultimate Money Friends Throwdown hours. Simply put, Money Friends are the key to multiplying your influence way beyond yourself. But how can we each flex our dollar power in community to influence others?

I've got a few ways you (and your Money Friends) can compound your impact. And you don't even need dollar bills to do it.

GRAB A MONEY FRIEND, MEET ME ON THE DANCE FLOOR!

Multiply Your Dollars

. . . Okay, so this first one might involve dollar bills. But they don't have to be yours. Maybe you're the most excited about the impact of actual money, and you feel the most powerful when you're helping to distribute cash where it's needed. You can multiply your dollar power by helping the folks around you to move their wallets, too.

If this sounds like your jam, grab a Money Friend and brainstorm:

$ How can we pledge to change the way we spend every day? How can we hold each other accountable to those plans; how can we celebrate our wins together?

$ How can we teach others what we've learned about budgeting, donating, mutual aid, or conscious spending? How can I help get the folks around me financially stable, too?

$ What causes are most important to us, and how can we financially support the organizers, educators, and collectives around us?

And if you're sitting here like, "'Kay, but what if we lichrally have. No. Dollars," there are so many ways to move other people's dollars for $Free.99. All you need is a lil' Wi-Fi.

When George Floyd and Breonna Taylor were murdered by police in 2020, folks ran to the internet to:

$ **Use social media to drive donations.** You and your Money Friends can shout about donation or mutual aid channels you learn about. That stuff actually works: According to a report by Classy.org, 59% of Generation X folks who have donated before were inspired to donate after seeing someone's social media post.

$ **Get creative for a cause.** 2020 saw folks offering their art skills to make custom portraits for people, asking folks for donations instead of birthday gifts, even creating long YouTube videos to collect advertising revenue—so that all money could go toward the cause of their choice.

$ **Side hustle for justice.** Remember our side-hustle tips in chapter 4? Combine your powers with Money Friends and hit up your community to offer your skills: you can photograph, babysit, virtually tutor, or offer tech skills in exchange for donation dollars.

Multiply Your Privileges

Now, maybe the circumstantial gawds have smiled upon you and your Money Friends; maybe you all happen to hold a bunch of power just being who you are. When you have a certain status or identity that makes moving through life a bit easier—as a voter, a documented person, an able-bodied person—your privilege is part of your wealth. And you can use your privileges to speak up for others and apply pressure to those who have financial power right in your neighborhood.

If this speaks to you and your Money Friends, have a brainstorm:

$ Are there ways we can show up for those who are more vulnerable, who can't physically risk their lives or their paycheck—say, at a protest or demonstration? Are there ways we can help with setup, admin, or marketing for an existing movement?

$ Are there opportunities around us to help hold local political leaders accountable in the way they spend the city budget— maybe showing up at a town hall or public budget hearing?

$ How can our group help friends and family understand

what's on the next ballot, and how certain laws affect their money lives? How can we help other folks learn about where our tax dollars go, and how to vote accordingly?

Privilege is powerful if used responsibly. We must use our privileges to center the financial needs of those we are advocating for, which requires listening before jumping into action.

Multiply Your Networks

Speaking of listening: calling all fellow hype-folks! Some of us are good at getting straight-up loud. Your ability to work your network can be a huge part of your wealth. You and your Money Friends can act as megaphones, amplifying calls for whatever financial help your cause needs, or starting financial justice conversations in the communities around you.

If you're tryna multiply your impact using your network, you might ask:

$ How can we get wealthier or well-connected folks to support our cause? Do any of us have access to workplace, alumni, or family connections—aka rich people—and can we influence them to open their wallets for our cause?

$ How can we use social media as a mic to teach other folks where to donate, how to organize, or what crappy companies we should divest from? How can we make it super easy or fun for friends to share our work?

$ How can we engage in conversations with our own friends and family about what we've learned, how we spend, and how we give? (Because talk about influence—any message can come through so much stronger when it's delivered from someone they already love and trust. Das you.)

We gotta combine a few lessons we've learned here: we can think about what our financial relationship is to the folks we're advocating for, and where the money power lies. We can use tools like social media to amplify and listen, always keeping in mind what dollar power your cause actually needs (and being careful our activism doesn't turn into clout chasing).

If you always keep the financial needs and goals of your community in the spotlight, you (and your Money Friends) can never go wrong.

Now, here's what's wild: I believe that we are at the very beginnings of a personal and global financial revolution. I know that by the time I finish this sentence, our political climate will have changed, the needs of marginalized and systemically excluded people will change, and so the way we need to respond with our dollars will change, too.

But one fact will never change, no matter what our financial climate looks like: this world needs you. Your Money Friends need you. Your cause needs a specific type of financial noise that you have the power to create.

To be honest? I'd love it if you took any of these tips to heart, but I don't actually care if you become a whole-a$$ financial activist or not. I'm not trying to get you to stomp around these streets (internet or otherwise), advocating loudly for change, if that's not what calls to you.

I care that you know one thing: whatever you have to give, and however you want to give it, there's a place for you (and your dollars) in any revolution. I care that you recognize the power you have in a world that literally profits off of telling you that you're powerless. I care that you know this in your bones: You can choose the impact you make on this world.

And I hope you get to knowin' this stuff soon, too, because this party truly isn't the same without you.

My job as Hype Woman is to simply keep the energy up. But the vibe in the room's starting to shift.

It's time for you to get up out of the audience. It's time for you to grab the mic.

WAIT, WHAT?

Y'know, I almost don't wanna give you a checklist here—learning to get down with financial activism is a lifelong lesson, and none of us get to say "Check! Done! I did my part forever, byeeee!" But just getting started can be hella intimidating, so let's review a few ways to begin your journey.

$ Give it a five-minute think: What kind of companies do you want to give your money to? What values does a brand have to show to win your dollar? (Check out our list on page 225 to start.)

$ Take a sec to look at the banks, investing institutions, or brands who currently take your money. Give 'em a Google to see if any shady news comes up. Do they pass your new value test? If no, how can you move your money toward what you believe in?

$ . . . And while you've got your bank accounts open, see if you can set aside Justice/Privilege/Community Care funds each month. Pick your cause for next month—and text a Money Friend about it. (Peek at page 230 for more.)

$ Gather your Money Friends and talk about what you can do now to multiply your dollar—start at page 244 and vote for which method sounds most fun to start with.

LAST SONG

Ugh. I hate how even the best parties have to come to an end.
I am always the last one on the dance floor. And there are a squi-
llion other money things that simply didn't fit; I could honestly
write seven thousand more pages. (I basically did, but we had to
cut 'em. Ask my editor.)

I've gotta wrap up my solo, but guess what? I'm passing the mic
foreal now. This next part is all you.

But lemme leave you with some final Hype Woman words
before you step into that spotlight.

Money is one of the few frickin' things that connects all
humans. (Besides . . . love or whatever.) It's what brought me to
you, right? And despite the fact that so many of us have felt shoved
out, shamed, and marginalized, I am living proof: we all belong in
the money world. We all deserve to know the rules of the money
game so we can change those rules on our terms. We all deserve
control of our own financial freedom. I fiercely believe we are
destined for more than just survival—and money
can help us live (and give) the way we want.

HELL YES

With all that in mind, we have to bring our whole identity—our culture, our families, our traumas, and our joys—into our money lives, because money has touched every. Single. Part. Your lived experiences make you an expert on your money life. What you have to say about money is not only hella valid—it's necessary.

Because here's the thing: there's someone in the crowd who's been waiting for you to get financially empowered and finally take the mic. Whether you're sharing your debt struggles with a friend, opening your family's first retirement fund, or protesting your city's budget, your dollar power could unlock financial freedom for others and literally save lives. My ultimate financial dream for you is said best by the legendary American novelist Toni Morrison: "If you are free, you need to free somebody else."

Like everything else in life, money is better when it's shared—both literally and emotionally. So the most financially powerful thing you can do now? Share your learnings. Take what you learned from this book and reinvest your new knowledge into your community. Let money change your life, and the lives of those around you, the way it changed mine.

(. . . Sorry, okay, in true Filipino fashion, saying goodbye takes me forty-five minutes—)

The mic is hot, my friend. This is your show now. Like any good Financial Hype Woman should, I'll be right behind you every step of the way. And that audience? They're vibing with you, too.

So speak up. Speak loud. I stole the aux cord for us. This is our money party now.

GLOSSARY

401(k): an investing retirement account that an employer may offer, where you and/or your employer can contribute money directly from your paycheck, usually after paying taxes.

529 Plan: an investing account specifically made to save for education. Typically, you don't pay taxes when you take the money out, but you must spend it on school-related stuff.

Avalanche Method: a loan payoff strategy in which you keep making your minimum payments on all your loans, but you put extra money toward the loan with the highest interest first. Technically, you're getting rid of your most "expensive" loan faster.

balance: how many dollars you have in a bank account, or how much you owe on a loan or credit card.

bonds: a type of investment that is a loan we give to a company or to the government. When you buy a bond, you're letting a company or government borrow your money, and they promise to give it back in a certain number of years, plus interest.

boycott: when many people refuse to buy from a certain brand until the brand gets their act together.

brokerage account: a bank account specifically for investing. You deposit your money, and a brokerage—aka, an investment middle-man company—invests the money for you.

budget: a system of personal rules that you set up to keep track of how you spend your money.

capital gains tax: a tax you typically have to pay after you sell an investment, based on how much profit you made (if you made any).

capitalism: an economic system in which everything needed to make products—like factories, land, oil, ships—is owned by private individuals and companies, instead of being owned by the government. The focus of capitalism is profit, profit, profit.

Certified Public Accountant / CPA: someone who earned a specific license to legally give accounting services—like tax help—to other people.

checking account: a kind of bank account you can open at most banks. Checking accounts are built for all-day, every-day use; you get a debit card to spend your money at stores and restaurants, and you can usually move money in and out of the account whenever you want.

compounding: when your interest earnings are added to your original amount, so your savings or investments keep growing over time. Think of a tiny snowball getting bigger as it rolls down a hill. (This unfortunately works the same way with debt and the amount you owe.)

consolidate: when you work with a company to negotiate your loans all into one big loan, and one monthly payment.

co-signer: an adult who shares responsibility with you on a loan, who legally agrees to make payments on your loan if, for some reason, you can't.

credit score: a number that basically tells banks and lenders how good you are at paying back debt. It's like a grade for your credit, typically given to us by three different companies called credit bureaus.

credit union: a financial institution that's not technically a bank; it's a not-for-profit cooperative whose members can borrow from each other at low rates.

custodial account: a bank account that someone eighteen years or older can open for someone under eighteen. Adults can open different kinds of custodial accounts—like savings, checking, or investment accounts—for younger folks. Usually, only the adult can move money in or out of the account.

default: when you've been delinquent or overdue on payments for a while—usually around 270 days or more. Most of the time, it means the loan company is so pissed about your late/missing monthly payments, they're making you pay the entire total right now.

deferment: pausing a federal loan because of a "qualifying" financial or personal issue (what "qualifies" depends on the lender). Depending on the type of loan, you may not need to pay interest while on deferment.

delinquency: when you're overdue for payment on a debt you owe. These bad boys show up on your credit report.

deposit: to put money into an account, usually by bringing cash to a bank or by transferring money between accounts online.

diversification: a fancy term for "having a lot of different kinds of investments, so that you don't have to worry too much if one type of investment fails."

divest: when we "break up" with a financial institution by selling our investments with them or withdrawing our funds.

Exchange Traded Funds / ETF: a type of investment very similar to mutual funds—you can spread your money out over an index, or even a specific industry—but unlike a mutual fund, where you pay a human to pick the investments and they can only trade during certain hours, you can buy or sell an ETF on your own and basically anytime.

financial aid: any type of money given or lent to help pay for education. This could include loans, work study, grants, scholarships, and more.

fintech: financial technology = fintech! This could be mobile apps, computer programs, or any other technology aimed toward money-related services.

fixed interest rate: an interest rate on a loan that will not change. It could stay the same for the entire time you have the loan or just for a fixed-rate portion of it, depending on your loan's terms.

forbearance: pausing a federal loan because of a "qualifying" financial or personal issue but, depending on the type of loan, you may still be responsible for interest while you're in forbearance.

Free Application for Federal Student Aid / FAFSA: a form that students who want to go to college in the US can fill out to see if they can receive financial aid from schools or the government.

gross income: income is how much money you make when you work, but as we learn on page 59, most of us get money taken out of our paycheck (for Adult-y things like taxes, Social Security, health insurance) before we get to take that money home. Gross income is the full amount you earned before that money was taken out.

High Yield Savings Account / HYSA: a savings account that offers a significantly higher than average interest.

index funds: a type of investment in which you can make one purchase and spread your money over different stocks and bonds—but(!) instead of being managed by a human, like a mutual fund, index funds follow an "index," or a list of companies that show how a general section of the stock market is doing all at once.

Individual Tax Identification Number / ITIN: a number you can receive from the Internal Revenue Service (IRS) to help you qualify to do things like open bank accounts or pay taxes. This is an alternative to a Social Security Number and can feel more secure for undocumented folks to use.

interest: money that banks either add to your savings account or add to your debt. Usually interest looks like a percentage, like 0.5%, which may be called "interest rate," "annual percentage yield" (APY), or "annual percentage rate" (APR).

investing: buying something—an object, a piece of a company, anything with value—in the hopes that it will be worth more in the future and can be sold for profit.

joint account: a type of bank account that you share with someone else. A person under eighteen can have a joint account with someone over eighteen and, typically, both people can move money in or out freely.

Land Tax: money that non-Indigenous people living in the US can pay to support the sovereign rights of the first peoples of the land we work and live on.

minimum payment: the smallest amount a lender says you can pay on a debt you owe without getting hit by any penalties or fees.

minimum wage: the lowest amount of money an employer can pay you, legally.

mutual aid: a social/financial framework based on the belief that, instead of relying on folks in power to help us, a community can work together to meet its own needs in order to disrupt power systems and create structural and systemic change.

mutual funds: an investment in which you can make one purchase and spread your money over hundreds of different stocks and bonds. Mutual funds are usually "actively managed," aka you pay a human to help you pick your investments.

net income: how much money you get to take home after all the Adult-y stuff (taxes, social security, health insurance, etc.) gets taken out of your paycheck.

overdraft fees: an amount of money you are charged if your bank account balance goes below $0.

portfolio: a collection of all the investments a person has.

robo-advisor: an online, artificial-intelligence-powered financial service that can help you invest without interacting with/paying other humans.

Roth IRA: a type of investing retirement account that any working adult can open, in which you can contribute money after paying taxes.

savings account: a bank account that is set up for keeping your money for a long time. Usually, you can only move money in and out of the account a limited number of times per month.

sinking fund: a strategy in which you save money in an account for a specific purpose—like car repairs, medical bills, or an upcoming vacation.

Snowball Method: a loan payoff strategy in which you put extra money toward paying off your smallest loan first (while still making your minimum payments on all your loans). That way, you can pay off that small debt quickly and get an emotional win ASAP.

Social Security: a government system in which the government gives you a paycheck each month when you retire or stop working. The idea is that when you're younger, part of your taxes go to a big Social Security pot for the whole country, and when you need it, you get paid from that same pot.

stock: a type of investment that represents a piece of a company. You can buy a stock and become a partial owner of that company, and the value of that stock can change according to how well the company is doing.

stock market: a general term used to talk about whether people are buying investments in a particular industry or country. (Not to be confused with the stock exchange, which is the actual in-person and online marketplace where people buy and sell stocks, like NASDAQ or the New York Stock Exchange.)

strike: when workers refuse to work under unfair conditions and hold back their dollar-earning power from their employer.

student loan: money we borrow to pay for school, and have to pay back later. We borrow either from the school itself, from the government, and/or from a private company.

taxes: money a government takes from businesses and citizens to pay for stuff we all share.

variable interest rate: an interest rate that could go up and down over time, which could change your monthly payments.

wealth gap: when one social group has more money, property, and investments than another group, on average.

withdraw: to take money out of an account, usually in the form of cash, a paper check, or a transfer between accounts online.

ACKNOWLEDGMENTS

I was born on, raised on, and wrote a majority of this book on the unceded ancestral homeland of the Ramaytush Ohlone peoples, who are the original inhabitants of the San Francisco Peninsula.

I pay an annual Yunakin Land Tax to support their fight for sovereign rights as first peoples of this land, and I encourage you all to do the same for the first peoples of the land around you! More on how to do this on page 238.

Okay, honestly, everything good in my life traces back to the simple fact that I was really well loved by my parents, Bema and Alex Anat. You're a couple of bad b*%#h immigrants from the Philippines who came to the Bay and overcame everything, and that's why this book exists. I will spend my whole life trying to thank you.

. . . Also, remember that time at Chevy's on El Camino, I was like eleven, and I said I wanted to be a writer and you were like, *No. Pediatrician.* And I cried? LMAO. HELLA FUNNY (in retrospect).

Tabia Yapp, my literally fearless agent: When I sent that first cold email with a line from *The Office*, I had no idea how ridonku-lously lucky I'd be to get a response. You have unlocked my wildest dreams, and you never fail to remind me of my worth. You are the cheat code.

Courtney Stevenson, the editor of my dreams, the massager of minds, the most patient doula of deadlines: You always advocated for me, for the book, for us. You taught me to trust myself as the unhinged captain of my own ship, and I'll never, ever forget it.

Monique Sterling, our magical illustrator and designer: You built a world even better than what my tangled brain could imag-ine. Erin Fitzsimmons, the art director with the patience of a thousand espressos: Thank you for never losing your sh*t when my Libra moon said, *k but what about...?* Karen Santos, your photog-raphy literally stopped the presses. What an honor to partake in your powerful magic. Lindsay Dabalos, you made me look and feel sparkly.

Extra jazz hands to the rest of the HarperCollins crew: Rose-mary Brosnan, Kristen Eckhardt, Erin DeSalvatore, Mark Rifkin, Laura Mock, Amy Ryan, Alexandra Rakaczki, Shannon Cox, Lau-ren Levite, Patty Rosati, and Mimi Rankin. It takes a village and OURS IS DOPE.

Anna N'Jie-Konte: Thank you for your time and expert CFP wizardess eye. Dr. Akilah Cadet, your sensitivity edit made this a more inclusive book, and your friendship makes me a better person. And a special thanks to Jonathan Cordero, PhD of the Association of the Ramaytush Ohlone for helping with our Land and Land Tax acknowledgment.

To this book's godparents: Tiffany Aliche, my first money idol, you've given me the keys to the kingdom in so many ways. Michelle

MiJung Kim, you've shown me the importance of sisterhood and softness as WOC authors. To late nights with Peggy Lee in our safe space, The Ruby. I'll stop lovingly calling it a cult when y'all stop making it so cozy and life-changing.

To my first readers, Kaitlin Menza, Devin Tomb (y'all, we're authors writing acknowledgments now!!!), Kara Perez, Jensen Luther: Thank you for holding my bb, for so lovingly giving your time and brains to push, prod, and hype me up. And special thanks to Peter Wagner, for taking such good care of me during my ugliest, most mouth-breathing manuscript days.

To my Textperts, Shani Tran, Daniella, Carter Cofield, Adina Appelbaum, Esq., Mauricio Castillo Ferri, Paco De Leon, Aja Dang, Amanda Holden, Dasha Kennedy, Yanely Espinal: This book (and my career) would be a stack of incoherent babble without you. Additional forehead kisses to Erin Lowry, Stefanie O'Connell, Jamila Souffrant, Chris Browning, Mandi Woodruff, all of my HellaHelpful instructors, everyone I've ever shared a stage or screen with. You were my first safe spaces in the money world. Marry me.

To my Open Mic contributors: You are the best part of my book and my career. My HellaHelpful members, all the OGs who've been around since @heyberna was wee: You gave me this life, and what an honor to keep building it with you.

Kristen Brillantes, you see me. I literally don't know what other creators do without the grounded sisterhood of someone like you. Joely Liriano, what an honor to have our work shaped by your sharp eye and your fierce protection of peace. Jeffrey, thank you for supporting us with enthusiasm and care.

Earnest Girl Who Loves Her Family Alert: Thank you, Ate Robie, my first idol, for your gentleness and your strength. Kuya

Jason, for teaching me how to hold a knife and how to spot a good man among boys. Mark . . . shut up. I always have and always will copy everything you do, and that's why I'm a MESS. Andrew . . . shut up. Watching you blossom into your true self has been incredible and cringe. Get it together. Jasmine, if you ever leave us, we are truly screwed. You're my sister forever. And to my uncles, especially Unks Leo and Uncle Jojo: You gave me my sense of humor. I want a refund. What an honor to be raised by you all.

Little Jas, Jordan, Jada, Isla, my babies: You are my most important people in the world. I'll spend forever trying to make this world suck less for you. As long as I stay your favorite auntie, cause if not, whole deal's off.

To Sam, Isa, Nada (and Owen and Georgie and Emi!), Franny, Kat, Eryne, Tiffany, Claire, Alex, Maria, KAB, Jackie, Branché, S'rah, Lec, Amir, Katie, Ning, Max, Ashley, Shani, Adonis: You are entitled to financial compensation. I love you with every inch of my deep-fried heart.

To every brown girl in South City and Daly City reading this— look, dude. Just look at what we're capable of.

And finally: to Lula, Lulu, Lola Magdalena. And every ancestor I haven't met (yet). Sniff kiss. Bless. Toodles. I hope you're watching us and thinking, "Yeah. It was worth it."